The Church We Carry

Other Abingdon Press Books by Will Willimon

Changing My Mind

Don't Look Back

Preachers Dare

Listeners Dare

Stories by Willimon

Will Willimon's Lectionary Sermon Resources Series

Fear of the Other

Who Lynched Willie Earle?

Pastor, Revised Edition

Holy Spirit (with Stanley Hauerwas)

Resident Aliens (with Stanley Hauerwas)

Incarnation

Sinning Like a Christian

Why Jesus?

This We Believe

Will Willimon

The Church We Carry

Loss, Leadership, and the Future of Our Church

Abingdon Press™

Nashville

THE CHURCH WE CARRY:
LOSS, LEADERSHIP, AND THE FUTURE OF OUR CHURCH

Copyright © 2025 by William H. Willimon

Library of Congress Control Number: 2025940122

ISBN: 978-1-7910-3715-4

MANUFACTURED IN THE UNITED STATES OF AMERICA

For John and Susan
In gratitude for your open hearts

On the outskirts of every agony sits some observant fellow who points.

—Virginia Woolf, quoted in frontispiece of
Who Lynched Willie Earle?:
Preaching to Confront Racism

Contents

Prelude

I was told not to write this book. Never has a church staff been ordered not to answer my emails, or people refuse to talk to me. A litigious leader of the breakaway Global Methodist Church warned that if I proceeded with this project, "As an attorney" he suspected that I might be committing "defamation and libel."

"Frankly, many of us are exhausted by this disaffiliation thing and are ready to turn the page. Wish you wouldn't bring it up," said more than one bishop.

"Global Methodist Elder," Jeffrey Rickman, after saying "you'd have to be crazy to be happy in a UMC" and dismissing me as "churlish," posted a long diatribe condemning this book. Nine months before it had been published.

A preacher urged to stop talking? Truth somebody wants hidden? Threats of litigation? Lucky for us preachers, Jesus never backed down from an argument, nor does he do silence: "Nothing is hidden that won't be exposed. Nor is anything concealed that won't be made known and brought to the light" (Luke 8:17).

Then Jesus warns, "Those who have will receive more, but as for those who don't have, even what they seem to have will be taken away" (8:18). Might the few treasured memories of my home church that I carry be purloined by what I learn?

In less than twelve months during 2023–2024, The United Methodist Church—once the largest Protestant denomination in the country—lost a third of its congregations. 7,766. Other mainline denominations had experienced schism in the preceding decades, but the scale and speed of United Methodism's declension was unprecedented. A seismic shock. Here is a memoir, a letter from a jilted lover, an exposé of a church fight, an account of what I learned about the disaffiliation of my well-remembered home congregation, an ecclesial Whodunit, a reflection upon the major dynamics within mainline Protestantism today, and an invitation to pastors, lay leaders, and members of today's church to learn from what once happened at my home church as they figure out how to be the church that we bear into the future.

A few years ago, PBS documented my moves from a biblical text to a sermon in context; TV at its most scintillating. Somebody decided the documentary ought to be accompanied by "A Conversation with Will Willimon,"[1] probing my background, influences, and history as a preacher. I quite naturally suggested filming at my home church. Senior Pastor Brian Gilmer welcomed the film crew into the chapel of Buncombe Street United Methodist Church. There I paid tribute to personalities, sermons, and events whereby the Trinity worked with one Methodist congregation to make me a spokesperson for God.

Months later, ever-gracious Brian invited me back to Buncombe Street, my tenth or twelfth visit over the years. When I asked about the challenges the congregation was bearing, Brian replied, "We are trying to dig out after the ravages of COVID, the lockdown, and all that. It would be great if you could remind folks why we really need them to come back to church!"

Thus I preached:

Being Saved at Buncombe Street

Matthew 4:17-22
January 30, 2022

Back in my day, you couldn't walk down Main Street on a Saturday without being accosted by a student from Bob Jones asking, "Are you saved?"

---

1. "A Conversation with Will Willimon," PBS, May 17, 2021, https://www.pbs.org/video/a-conversation-with-will-willimon-igqfmm/.

I was fairly sure that whatever answer I gave would be wrong, but on the corner of Main and McBee, age ten, when asked, "Kid, are you saved?" as a longtime citizen of Greenville, I was locked and loaded. "I'm a member of Buncombe Street Methodist. Just joined last week."

"Having your name on a church roll, especially that church, isn't being saved," he responded.

"Tell it to Dr. R. Bryce Herbert," I scoffed as I continued toward the Fox Theater.

Thirteen years later, at Yale Divinity School, I learned what the church taught throughout the centuries, extra Ecclesiam nulla salus. No salvation outside the church. Sounded harsh, exclusionary. . . .

But then I remembered Buncombe Street. I realized that "no salvation outside the church" is the humble recognition that salvation in Jesus Christ is a group phenomenon. As John Wesley said, "There's no such thing as a solitary Christian. Salvation in Christ is always social." We will be saved as a group (aka, Buncombe Street) or saved not at all.

Which brings me to this Sunday's Scripture, Matthew 4:17-20:

From that time Jesus began to announce, "Change your hearts and lives! Here comes the kingdom of heaven!"

As Jesus walked alongside the Galilee Sea, he saw two brothers, Simon, who is called Peter, and Andrew, throwing fishing nets into the sea, because they were fishermen. "Come, follow me," he said, "and I'll show you how to fish for people."

From the first, Jesus assembles, congregates, and convenes a group (not the brightest candles in box) and sends them out to do what he wants done in the world. Church.

My sermon has but two points: (1) Jesus not only comes to us, Jesus enlists us. He doesn't just save, he calls. (2) Whatever Jesus wants to do in the world, he chooses to do it not alone. He refuses to save us without enlisting us. Jesus the Delegator, Assembler. Convener, Congregator. It's called church. Salvation (being made right with God) is a group phenomenon.

Be honest: It isn't that easy being a follower of Jesus with his constant insistence that we love our neighbor, turn the other cheek, sacrifice, give. But maybe the biggest challenge of following Jesus is his demand that we follow in the company of other followers of Jesus! It's called church. . . .

As bishop, I never had a preacher call it quits because of Jesus. You'd think they would say, "Jesus is just too demanding! Every time I read Scripture, Jesus raises the bar! Can't take it."

No, the reason that clergy call it quits is not Jesus. It's you. *The laity. Love Jesus but can't stand his friends! . . .*

I know you've been through tough time with COVID. Hey, with all the work you must do to get kids off to school on weekdays, then get to the office, there's no energy left for church. After being pent-up for so long, wary of being in crowds, you feel anxious about being in a group.

Here's my point: Jesus doesn't care! To you he says, as he said to them in all their fears, reservations, brokenness, and temptations to fly solo: "Follow me!" How? Together!

There's no way I'd be following Jesus today without Buncombe Street.

These days, when asked, "Are you saved?" I tell this story.

When I was ten, my mother deposited me at Buncombe Street Methodist every Thursday afternoon for the church membership class. I retained nothing about Methodism from that class. My confirmation occurred not in the church sanctuary on Sunday but rather in the back parking lot on Thursday before Holy Week. On Palm Sunday we were to be joined to the church. The bulletin that Sunday was to feature a photo of the class lined up on the front steps of Buncombe Street.

Thursday, I was greeted by the Commander of Confirmands: "Where's your tie?"

I froze.

"You were told to wear a tie. We're taking the confirmands' photo. There's a photographer—a professional. Dr. Herbert is to have his picture taken with the class—the preacher." She waved her hand over the assembled righteous. "Every boy has a tie. Even Stanley Starnes. See? You were told."

Words failed. I wheeled around and dashed out the door to the back parking lot. I would post myself at the preacher's parking space, head him off, confess my sin, and humbly bow out of the picture.

Sure enough, there was Dr. Herbert, pulling his light-blue Plymouth into the space. I breathlessly ran up and blurted, "Dr. Herbert, you don't know me but I'm William Willimon, and I didn't hear that we were supposed to have a tie, or I forgot, or maybe my mother didn't tell me, and I don't want to be in the picture anyway and . . ."

Dr. Herbert, with his stained glass bass voice, replied, "Tie? Why would you be wearing a tie? I am wearing a tie because I'm a pastor and I am forced to wear a tie. I'm unaware that you have had theological training."

All I've had is this dumb class.

"Are you not preparing yourself for membership in The Methodist Church?" he continued.

"Yessir."

"Well, son, I know more about these matters than anyone present, and I'm certain that there are no requirements in Methodism for ties to be worn in order to join the church. No record of our Lord ever having worn a tie, and I know Scripture," he muttered.

"Come along. The whole point of these ceremonials is to put you in the picture."

Dr. Herbert led me back into the darkened hall toward the primary classroom, where the others were detained by their keeper.

"Everyone's here," reported the woman in charge. "Nearly everyone has dressed for the photograph, as they were told. Even Stanley Starnes."

My heart stopped.

"What a beautiful group!" exclaimed Dr. Herbert. "I have one request before we go out and take our place on the church steps. Boys, please, no ties on a Thursday. Only I can wear a tie in church on a weekday. Such are the rules of our Connection. You may wear them if you must on Sunday. Please remove your ties. Let's take that picture."

God is like Dr. Herbert, without the Plymouth.

The morning after handing over this sermon, I received an email from Wiley Cooper, classmate back at Wofford College, now retired United Methodist minister:

From: Wiley Cooper
Sent: Monday, March 21, 2022 7:13 AM
To: Will Willimon
Subject: Called to Reconciliation

As one who has known you, read your books and sermons, and followed your ministry for many years I was deeply disappointed, as I was in your recent sermon at Buncombe Street UMC.

. . . you never once even mentioned LGBTQ+ exclusion, which is among the most critical sins of the church in our time. . . . In your sermon to Buncombe Street, you gave a beautiful, emotionally stirring, theologically well-grounded sermon, but in a church which is preparing to leave the UMC over the issue of LGBTQ+ inclusion, you again never explicitly mentioned it. . . .

When will you "come out of the closet," Will? Isn't it time for you to stand clearly and unabashedly for once and for all instead of speaking in code that can only be deciphered and applauded by those already convinced? How about just one of your many books on the subject of the biblical and theological grounding for inclusion of LGBTQ+ into full membership and shared leadership in the church of Jesus Christ and especially the UMC?

I love you; have for years. You have taught me much about preaching and leadership. I have unabashedly used much from your sermons (with attribution) all through my ministry. I knew Patsy at Trinity before you did, and love her too. But I am really disappointed in my old friend and often mentor.

Grace, Peace, Hope, Love and Faithful Resistance,

Wiley Cooper

I tossed back a frantic response:

On Mar 21, 2022, at 11:54 AM, Will Willimon wrote:

Wiley,

I'm shocked, and a bit pissed, that no one managed to mention to me, in an entire weekend at BS, that they are actually thinking about bolting. Didn't know that. In my retreat on Saturday I got into an argument with the Seekers group and I think I defended L,G,B,T,Q inclusion quite well, if I do say so.

I didn't mention the matter in my Sunday sermon because it didn't seem related to my text, but looking back, I could have, and indeed would have, had I known BS was leaning in the direction you indicate. . . .

If it's any encouragement, I served a UMC congregation here in Durham for a year. . . . I led them toward being a Reconciling Congregation. . . .

After the coming separation, the UMC and its churches will definitely be the only Wesleyan place for those who are committed to full inclusion. I therefore think it's important to stay UMC and argue for that. . . .

Thanks for your letter. Sorry I disappointed.

Will

By Friday, a friend since the fifth grade—third-generation leader of Buncombe Street, jeweler, businessman retired—John Redmond called: "Well, looks like there is a group hell-bent to take us out of The UMC. Been having secret meetings for months, unknown to most of us old guard. We're scurrying to counter their misinformation. Got any advice?"

True, the only comment I remembered, after two days with the Seekers, was the guy who said he had joined Buncombe Street because, "We were lifelong Episcopalians but when they ordained that queer bishop, we said, 'That's enough.'"

Spurred on by the shocking news of Buncombe Street's secretive schismatics, I began months of interviewing United Methodists around the country as fodder for my book *Don't Look Back: Methodist Hope for What Comes Next*, my attempt to give United Methodists a defense of our church amid schism. I conducted video interviews with a couple hundred United Methodist pastors, talked to dozens of UMC bishops, and spent a score of weekends in United Methodist churches. Then I wrote *Don't Look Back*, my broadside against the newly formed Global Methodist Church, my biblical and theological defense of United Methodism, and my ideas for how to work renewal in our congregations.

Among those who ignored *Don't Look Back* was the church that made me a Methodist.

Leave Taking

I never meant to be Methodist. Didn't have to. My forebears allegedly founded octagonal McBee Chapel Methodist Church in the 1830s. (On the back of the second pew to the rear right, you can still see ROy ROjERs carved by my brother Bud one Sunday as my mother dozed.) Riding home from church, transfixed by a passing field overcome with kudzu (the one crop that cooperated with the Willimons), I asked, "Am I a Christian?"

Mother answered, "Of course. And Methodist, by virtue of your father's family. You were christened in Mama's living room—after the preacher consumed a fried chicken, three ears of corn, and a peck of okra. Sad man. Vanderbilt Phi Beta Kappa but, because he was a Methodist preacher, none of his five children could afford college," she sighed. . . .

"But what if I don't want to be a Methodist?" I persisted.

"That will not be possible," she replied.

—Accidental Preacher: A Memoir

"I understand things have worked out well at your home church," chortled the bishop, over a plate of fried shrimp. "The group who wanted to stay UMC have found a home at Trinity across town. I hear it's packed on Sundays."

"The disaffiliation of Buncombe Street is more complicated," snarled I, across Cajun catfish. "Loyal Methodists have been hurt. A bunch of folks feel The UMC let them down."

In either heartfelt encouragement or snarky sarcasm, the bishop said words to me few have dared: "So why don't you write a book about it?"

In the parking lot afterward, one of our lunchtime companions, a retired UMC district superintendent, grasped my lapel: "They gave away a wonderful church that I spent a decade of my life to lead. A couple of hundred United Methodists voted out by those who broke their vows to support the church. Now the bishops want us to stop whining, get over our grief, and forget that they gave away the store. I beg you. Speak up for us. Tell our story. Write that book."

The next morning I began calling people whom I remembered from growing up in Greenville and at Buncombe Street. I also contacted fellow clergy in the South Carolina Conference whom I knew over the years of my ministry. "I'm trying to understand how my home church, two hundred years Methodist, second largest in the South Carolina Conference, decided to exit the denomination. Can you help me?"

After a few weeks of conversations, I began more systematically contacting people whose names were given to me when I asked, "Who do I need to talk to in order better to understand what went down at Buncombe Street?" By late August 2024, I was at work on this book, which is based upon what I learned and my reactions to what I was told. In the first weeks of conversations, with only one exception, people graciously conversed with me. Those who had led the disaffiliation were proud of their accomplishment; those who felt wronged by what was done or left undone were grateful that at last somebody was telling their story. Few asked that our conversations be "off the record." Here goes.

All the way back in 2009 I had been invited back from bishoping in 'Bama to preach the 175th Anniversary of the church where I met Jesus (and the hundredth anniversary of the church's Boy Scout Troop Nine, where I had met a variety of unseemly adolescent behaviors). Fifty years after I left Buncombe Street for Yale Divinity School, 175 years after a group of pious Wesleyan women (and one man) plotted to birth Greenville Methodist Church in Martha Turpin's living room in her big two-story house on the corner of Main and North, I preached in the same pulpit from whence I first overheard good news about God:

Buncombe Street, Through Faith Colored Glasses
November 15, 2009
175th Anniversary of
Buncombe Street United Methodist Church
Acts 2:43-47

Luke's Gospel was such a success, somebody said to Luke what nobody ever said to me: "Why don't you write another book?"

And Luke did just that, a second volume, the Acts of the Apostles, as if to say, "All that crucifixion, resurrection commotion caused by Jesus didn't end with Jesus—it continues even today in the church." Of course, by the time Luke wrote Acts, that church was nearly as old as Buncombe Street, so Luke was looking back on the first days. And you know how we often look back through "rose-colored glasses."

A sense of awe came over everyone [in First Church Jerusalem]. God performed many wonders and signs through the apostles. All the believers were united and shared everything. They would sell pieces of property and possessions and distribute the proceeds to everyone who needed them. Every day, they met together in the temple and ate in their homes. They shared food with gladness and simplicity. They praised God and demonstrated God's goodness to everyone. The Lord added daily to the community those who were being saved. (Acts 2:43-47)

Wow. That's quite a church. A church where every Sunday there were miracles, where everybody sold what they had and gave it to the poor, where every covered dish supper was a love feast, a church that grew in numbers. Wow. This passage comes right after Luke's report of Pentecost, just after Easter. It's like Luke is saying, "You want proof of the Resurrection? You want undeniable evidence that the Holy Spirit really descended upon ordinary people turning them into saints? Here it is: the history of First Church Jerusalem, a church of miracles, amazing growth, and 100 percent giving to apportionments."

Wish I could have been the pastor of that church. . . .

Back in 1965, Mr. A. M. Moseley (I still remember him, the prototypical Southern gentleman) published The Buncombe Street Methodist Story.

Page 89, there I am, front row, in the grainy photo of the Methodist Youth Fellowship. Mr. Moseley has been a big help with this sermon.

Our church was built on land given by Vardry McBee, who donated land with but one stipulation—that we promise never to bury anybody in our front yard. We have kept that promise, I think. In 1873, when a fine new building was dedicated, Mr. Moseley reports an eyewitness saying, "The weather most satisfactory, the sun shining in sympathy with the day, showered bright and joyous rays." (But when the church was short on the final payment for construction, Pastor Meynardie had all doors locked until donations closed the gap. Five persons gave a hundred dollars each and dinner was served.) By the way, on that glorious day, Bishop Doggett preached for over an hour, but Mr. Moseley says that nobody minded the bishop's verbosity because the sermon was "brilliant."

Mr. Moseley picked 1889 as the grandest year in our church's first century. After a revival by a talented Presbyterian evangelist, Buncombe Street experienced a spike in membership and giving. That same year Rev. W. A. Rogers proudly reported that "dram drinking and profanity" were "not common" among the membership of Buncombe Street, a boast that I'm sure your pastor, Brian Gilmer, could make even today.

"Our church, without a doubt, has been blessed with the best ministers," said Mr. Moseley. All had "that rare gift of oratorical persuasion to lift some members at times to such spiritual transfiguration that they feared to put their feet on earth again." Hmm. I remember my mother's evaluation of one of those preacher's sermons (on our way home after Sunday service) as remarkably different from Mr. Moseley's.

Only rarely does charitable Mr. Moseley admit to some less-than-glorious moments in Buncombe Street's past. In 1892 a financial crunch required the cessation of the $200 salary for paid singers. The board asked them to accept a slightly lower salary; the paid choir took a walk. In 1912, Dr. Mark Carlisle, in a letter to the congregation, said that even though he had been sent to Buncombe Street to build a new sanctuary, he was fed up with the constant bickering and therefore had asked the bishop to move him. In 1915 the Rev. B. F. Kilgo reported that Buncombe Street was a place of "aloofness and indifference" to newcomers in the congregation and if the board invited Evangelist McLendon to do a revival (Kilgo abhorred McLendon)

Kilgo would be absent. When the church fathers spitefully refused to build a garage for Rev. Kilgo's new car, he built one himself. When he was forced to move in November of 1919, Kilgo said he wouldn't leave until the church paid for the garage—$25. It was worth it to get that quarrelsome parson out of Greenville, groused one member of the board.

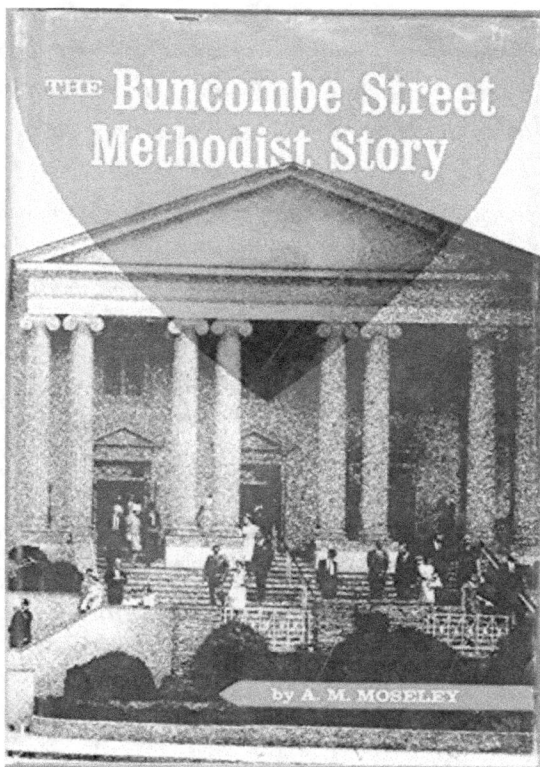

Mr. Moseley tantalizingly notes that in its first seventy-five years Buncombe Street retained only a couple of preachers more than two years. Out of sixty-seven pastors, only thirteen managed to endure Buncombe Street four years or longer. If everything was so sunny in the early Buncombe Street, how come so few preachers wanted to stay for the fun?

I'm not accusing saintly Mr. Moseley of lying, but I do suspect him of joining St. Luke in remembering the history of the church through rose-colored glasses. Or perhaps it's more accurate to say that both Luke and Mr. Moseley look through "faith-colored glasses." What you get, in the Acts of the Apostles or in Mr. Moseley's The Buncombe Street Methodist Story *is church through the eyes of faith.*

> Many miracles were done by the apostles. All who believed were together. They sold their possessions and distributed the income to anyone in need.

That's not a false view of church. It's what you see when you look at church sub specie aeternatis, *church as God sees church, church remembered in faith. The Letter to the Hebrews (Heb 11:1) defines "faith" as "the reality of what we hope for, the proof of what we don't see."*

Vardry McBee was not only the man who helped birth Buncombe Street; he was also the state's largest slaveholder. But how do you read that? That this church was birthed as beneficiary of terrible social evil or that God almighty takes our wrong, and brings good out of our bad?

It all depends on how you look at it.

This church, like any that has ever been, including Luke's First Church Jerusalem, is what you get in the glorious divine descent of Holy Spirit into grubby human muck and mire. This is not only the place where Mrs. Cureton handed me my first Bible but also where Stanley Starnes slugged me after Sunday school. Maybe the Holy Spirit was implicated in both of those events.

Thank God we've got a Savior who doesn't wait until we get it all together, until we are all cleaned up and spotless and honest about our history before he comes to us. . . .

I was invited back to Buncombe Street years ago. I was thrilled to see one of my old Sunday school teachers.

"Larry, thank you for what you meant to me back in the ninth grade. I will never forget that Sunday school class."

Larry responded, "Yea, I'll never forget it either, no matter how hard I try."

What? "I told Dr. Cook, I don't know nothin' about teenagers. I'm not good with the Bible. Get somebody else. Cook wouldn't take no for an answer (he had too much dirt on me so I was afraid of him). A miserable year. You kids wanted to talk more about sex than the Bible. It was awful."

"Er, uh, I don't remember any of that. I just remember getting a lot closer to God because of your class."

"I guess it's all in how you look at it," said Larry.

It was a Buncombe Street, body of Christ sort of moment. Larry was right. When it comes to church, this church or any other, it's how you look at it. Often I look at my church and see a declining, bickering, back-biting, boring all-too-human institution bent on its own demise. St. Paul looks at us and says, "You are the body of Christ!" You're the form Jesus has taken in the world. Jesus looks at his rag-tag group of disciples and says, "I'm going to take back what belongs to me—guess who's going to do it for me?"

It's all in how you look at it. . . .

After preaching this sermon, I stood in Buncombe Street's cramped narthex, just inside the door atop the limestone steps, and greeted folks at my homecoming. In a dozen handshakes and embraces, sixty years at Buncombe Street passed before me. Then, toting my robe (once worn by Bishop Kenneth Goodson) and my green stole (sewn by my mother) I headed for the vestry. I got no farther than the end of the second pew from the last, right-side aisle.

I stopped, transfixed by involuntary memory.

In that very spot (must have been the fall, '63) I was waylaid by Mr. J. B. Orders, ancient, revered, once feared, now frail, founder of Orders Mattress Company. I had just delivered to the Sunday evening Faithful Few a report on the doings of the Methodist Youth Fellowship trip to Junaluska; district youth rally at a church across town; not one, but two hot dog suppers for missions; study of the journeys of Paul with plywood map and differently colored lights for each of Paul's trips.

"Son, sit for a moment," said Mr. Orders, ominously.

"You are gifted."

"Thank you," I mumbled.

"I hope you have been thinking about college?"

"Yessir. I have. Not that I know where but, I…"

"College costs a lot of money. That's why I never got there. God has plans for you. Everybody knows that. The church needs good preachers. You should apply to whatever school you like. I'll gladly cover the cost of your college."

Mr. Orders stood, gathered his things, and walked out with Mrs. Orders into the evening cool. On the way home, I told my single-parent, just above the poverty line, Greenville High School home economics teacher mother what Mr. Orders had told me.

She responded, "What a nice thing for Mr. Orders to say. I hope, from what I hear of his business dealings, that with what I'm saving, we won't need to impose on his generosity. Still, you should be flattered by such encouragement."

Flattered was an inadequate description for what I felt.

If you ever visit now-renamed Buncombe Street Methodist Church, stand for a moment at the end of the second-from-last pew, on the right. Take off your shoes. That's holy ground.

My second year at Yale Divinity, in 1969, I took a graduate course with the great Southern historian C. Vann Woodward, just after he published *The Burden of Southern History.* Woodward told us that the history we Southerners bear was a burden that made us special among Americans. And a lifetime assignment. The Southern past could be a wonderful antidote to American exceptionalism, hubris, and naivete that had led us into disasters like the then-current Vietnam War. Only the South knew what it was to lose a war and be occupied by a foreign power. (My paper for Woodward was a study of the diary of a Freedman's Bureau officer in Greenville right after "The Woaher.") We were also the only part of the USA to be caught red-handed participating in and murderously defending a vast social evil.

Trouble was, we had lied about the burden of Southern history, attempting to unburden ourselves and get the past off our backs through the "myth of the lost cause," fantasies of past racial harmony, and other misrepresentations. "All Southern history, including mine, written before 1960, is not only dated but also wrong," declared Woodward. "If you grew up Southern, you are forced by your peculiar past to be an historian."

I added, under my breath, "If you are white, native Southern it also helps to believe in a God who loves to forgive and to save sinners."

Looking back over the course of my intellectual life, I see the influence of Woodward. We are not easily unburdened of the history we bear.

Rather than deceive ourselves about the past, the God who receives sinners and shares their table (Luke 15) also enables us to tell the truth of our past. Every Sunday, when we confess our sin, we acknowledge ourselves as sinners who, though uncomfortable with and (left to our own devices) incapable of candor, by the grace of God, can be truthful.

The history I bear from my home church can only be told straightforwardly with help from the One who is not only the way and the life but also the truth (John 14:6) and who got into all manner of trouble for receiving and partying with the likes of South Carolinians (Luke 15).

————————

So how did a reasonably content, nearly two-centuries-old congregation come to sever with our Connection? (That's how Methodists used to refer to ourselves, Mr. Wesley's "connexion," a network of interconnected congregations older than the denomination.) What—and pray tell who— led a loyal, rather placidly but still fully participating United Methodist congregation to break with the church family that gave it birth?

Methodist Youth Fellowship, 1961-62.

Even while I preached my 2009 sermon full of rose-tinted reminiscence and Mr. Moseley's affectionate history of Buncombe Street, events were unfolding behind closed doors throughout The UMC. My rose-colored glasses were about to be ripped off by what I discovered about the church that discovered me.

By the way, that's me, front row, bottom (lowly high school sophomore), third from right, peering out at the world beyond the church, as depicted in Mr. Moseley's *The Buncombe Street Methodist Story*:

Well, I guess you heard. Those nice, middle-of-the-road (sometimes to the point of mediocrity), Christian but not showy, evangelical-ish but not fanatical Methodists are getting a divorce. For the first time in a century, United Methodism is fracturing.

Sure, there had always been conservative critics within The UMC, but for the first time in history, those critics not only threatened to leave but also demanded to take church property with them. Worse, the bishops and General Conference of The UMC helped them do it.

Back in 1966, a couple of years before I graduated from college, Charles Keysor, a pastor in Elgin, Illinois, published a small magazine, *Good News*, in which he came out swinging against creeping liberalization in "Methodist officialdom and annual conference and national levels."[1] Before I became persona non grata at *Good News* I published a number of articles therein and was even featured in living color on the cover with Bob Wilson after our broadside, *Rekindling the Flame: Strategies for a Vital United Methodism*.

Ah, those golden days when I was the darling of the conservatives.

When Methodists first noticed that we were suffering massive losses, evangelicals claimed that the loss was due to the bungling of misguided liberals. No reputable study indicated that to be true; the decline seems mostly attributable to generational changes in church-going practices, led by my generation, the baby boomers. The birthrate among mainline, liberal Christians is lower than among conservative evangelicals; make of that what you want. Losses accelerated when our children grew up and found they could do without church. White flight from the major

---

1.   Cited in Russell E. Richey, Kenneth E. Rowe, and Jean Miller Schmidt, *The Methodist Experience in America: A History* (Abingdon Press, 2010), 503–04.

cities during the 1960s and 1970s devastated Methodism's aging, urban churches. Our accommodated, congenial but not too strongly committed, mainline Christian liberalism was no match for secular sociological pressures. In the face of the world's challenges, we went limp.

Buncombe Street was one of the few downtown United Methodist churches that found a way to entice white suburbanites to trek back into town for church. "You are in the top 5 percent of all Methodist urban churches," I would praise them every time I visited, though I have no idea where I got that stat.

Back at the United Methodist General Conference of 2004, James Heidinger, president of the misnamed *Good News*, got the separatist ball rolling with his proclamation of the bad news that "institutional separation is all but inevitable." If we couldn't have a no-fault divorce, then somehow we've got to find a way of "requiring the revisionists to depart." Push out the progressives who are destroying our church.

My friend Bill Henson, president of The UMC Confessing Movement, added, "I believe the time has come when we must begin to explore an amicable and just separation to free both sides from our cycle of pain and conflict [that will] protect the property rights of churches and the pension rights of clergy."

That same year, as soon as I got to North Alabama as bishop (Bill had retired to Huntsville), first thing I did was to seek out Bill to plead, "Please stop talking divorce! We need your voice and vision. Don't abandon us liberals!" The week before Bill and I were to meet, he died.

Denominational waters were increasingly turbulent. The floodgates opened at the ill-considered 2019 Special Session General Conference. After decades of wrangling over same-sex unions, whether or not to recognize the Lord's call of LGBTQIA+ folks to ordained ministry, some bishops got the bright idea, "Enough! Let's settle once and for all if the Lord wants us openly to include LGBTQIA+ persons in our churches," overlooking the thousands who were already serving in The UMC and also implying that the Holy Spirit would agree to limit his, her, or their disruptive machinations to the boundaries established by a majority vote of The UMC General Conference. The church capitulated to the biblically/theologically indefensible notion that somehow resolving the debate over sexual orientation issues was the most important issue facing The UMC.

The headline of my post–General Conference report in *The Christian Century* said it all: "The Methodist Mess in St. Louis." Once again, The UMC voted (this time, by a rapidly shrinking majority) to retain the *Book of Discipline*'s restrictions against ordaining gay clergy or performing same-sex marriages.

There, that settles it. Now will you promise never to bring up again matters that make us uncomfortable or expose "united" as the wrong sobriquet for the gaggle of Christians Christ has assembled as The UMC?

While those terrified by the prospect of LGBTQIA+ inclusion (Asbury Seminary, the Wesleyan Covenant Association [WCA], The Institute on Religion and Democracy, Methodists mainly in the Southeast and Texas, and the ghost of my seventh-grade Sunday school teacher) were high-fiving one another at having "won" the vote in Saint Louis to retain the *Discipline*'s restrictive language, many conservatives yet trembled.

Why? The WCA did the numbers. By the next quadrennial gathering, they were sure to be voted down on the one issue that they had made the most important issue in The United Methodist Church, the single issue that would cause them to walk, all the while protesting that this was not their only issue.

In the waning hours of the St. Louis debacle, even as the hall was being prepped for a monster truck show, amid the anguished cries of "Progressives" and LGBTQIA+ advocates and allies in rainbow stoles, an unlikely pair of bedfellows went to the mic and made a motion that would allow those who were outraged by the "traditional" stance of The UMC to leave. ¶2553 was approved. For the first time in history, the historic trust clause would be waived and the few pesky progressive United Methodist congregations could leave the denomination, taking all of a congregation's stuff with them.

The trust clause? In 1750, John Wesley had three lawyers craft deeds for Methodist preaching houses in England. These deeds would serve as models for all future deeds for the People Called Methodist. By having the annual conference hold a congregation's property in trust, Wesley believed that sound preaching and teaching would be ensured in every location. In 1796, under the leadership of first bishops Francis Asbury and Thomas Coke (under whose statues I had to pass every Sunday at Duke Chapel), a "model deed" was adopted by the General Conference for Methodists in America. The trust clause first appeared in the 1797 *Book of Discipline.*

While the local church owns the property, the trust clause requires that the property be "used, kept, and maintained as a place of divine worship of the United Methodist ministry and members of The United Methodist Church: subject to the Discipline, usage, and ministerial appointments of said Church as from time to time authorized and declared by the General Conference and by the annual conference within whose bounds the said premises are situated."

The trust clause didn't just protect and hold in trust the material fruit of the sacrifices and generosity of generations who built Methodist churches; it was a legal embodiment of a core Wesleyan conviction: "connectionalism." There's no such thing as a stand-alone, independent Methodist church that can do ministry or believe in Jesus any way they please.

Shared mission, gospel, and accountability hold United Methodist churches together as the denomination partners with the local church in maintaining and protecting the congregation's property. As bishop, I had to approve any sale, lease, indebtedness, or extensive renovation of congregational holdings. I also had a fiduciary responsibility to the communion of Methodist saints to do all I could to protect and encourage into the future the congregations their sacrifices had built.

The deed to Greenville Methodist Church, precursor of more alluringly named Buncombe Street (I would love to know what prompted the name change in 1892; Mr. Moseley's *Buncombe Street Story* doesn't tell) was executed on October 11, 1832. Therein is the "trust clause" for all to see. From its inception, Buncombe Street has been owned—pulpit, pew, and hymnal—by the denomination.

When in the 1990s, theologically conservative United Methodists moved from debate over the denomination's left-leaning tendencies to open discussion of splitting from the denomination, of course they wanted to take congregational property with them. The trust clause stood in their way, just as Wesley, Asbury et al. intended.

Some of the greatest spiritual accomplishments in Methodism were aided by the trust clause. Nobody believes that South Carolina United Methodists would have successfully racially integrated if they hadn't been prodded to do so by the trust clause, functioning exactly as Methodism meant.

And when some demagogic, out-of-control pastor attempted to purloin his congregation and go independent, nondenominational, he was removed from The UMC and the congregation continued to worship God in the Wesleyan way as connected Methodists, thanks to the trust clause.

Then the special-called General Conference of 2019 passed ¶2553. "Disaffiliation of a Local Church Over Issues Related to Human Sexuality."

Citing only one issue, "the current deep conflict within The United Methodist Church around issues of human sexuality," ¶2553 declared that, for the first time in history, local churches "shall have a limited right, under the provisions of this paragraph, to disaffiliate from the denomination for reasons of conscience regarding a change in the requirements and provisions of the Book of Discipline related to the practice of homosexuality or the ordination or marriage of self-avowed practicing homosexuals." Terms like "reasons of conscience" and "disaffiliate" had never been heard among Wesleyans. Nobody has ever pledged to "affiliate" with a United Methodist church and the whole point of *The Book of Discipline* is to ensure that Methodists refuse to entrust their souls either to unaided human reason or to dodgy human conscience.

No Scripture was cited in this motion that led to ¶2553 because the notion of allowing (encouraging?) a group of fellow Christians to leave our fellowship is alien to biblical faith. The trust clause was being circumvented, and progressive Methodists were being coaxed to leave the denomination and take church assets with them.

The process for "disaffiliation" in ¶2553 enabled a local church to leave and "to retain its real and personal, tangible and intangible property" while "the applicable annual conference shall release any claims that it may have under ¶2501 and other paragraphs of The Book of Discipline of The United Methodist Church commonly referred to as the trust clause."

The General Conference was (shockingly) relieved at the prospect of hurt, angry, "progressive" congregations leaving the connection, taking assets with them (which no one in the present congregation had built and paid for). Farewell LGBTQIA+ agitators. Good riddance.

I stood in the lobby, repeating what I, as a pastor, had said over the years to any disagreeing, disagreeable member (and there were many) who contemplated leaving my congregation: "Don't leave! Stay and fight! We'll be less church without you! I need you to help me be a better preacher!"

Turns out that just about no progressive congregations left. In one of the greatest ironies of Methodist history, the Wesleyan Covenant Association and its progeny (the nascent Global Methodist Church), knowing that they had "won" the battle but were sure to lose the war over the retention of restrictive Disciplinary language, hopped on ¶2553 as a means of exiting the denomination, taking church property with them. By a mere two-thirds vote of the members of the congregation present, a church could leave, seizing the legacy of the congregation's real estate, inherited, not purchased by the current members, including *United Methodist Hymnals*, endowments, folding metal chairs, needlepoint pew cushions, expired copies of *The Upper Room*, and the abandoned casserole dishes in the downstairs left closet of the church kitchen.

A two-thirds vote proved to be an absurdly low percentage for leave-taking. Nobody seemed bothered about the fate of those who "lost" a congregational election. A church is allowed to change its identity even if a third of the congregation didn't want to break their membership vows and stay UMC? My Baptist buddies mocked the ineptitude of Methodists taking congregational votes even when we had no history, or skill, in doing so.

Never mind that ¶2553 was designed exclusively for the purpose of exiting progressives, or that it should have been ruled unconstitutional by the Judicial Council the moment it hit the floor, or that it was based upon faulty, non-Wesleyan, (dare I say) nonbiblical reasoning.

Conservatives purloined ¶2553 as their get-out-of-the-denomination free pass. The Global Methodist Church was born. Although they had no beef with the denomination's stand against "the practice of homosexuality or the ordination or marriage of self-avowed practicing homosexuals" (having fought for and "won" it), conservatives suspected that still lurking in United Methodism were those who disagreed with them. If the progressives were allowed to go and take their stuff, *which they didn't,* we who once styled ourselves Evangelicals, who then became "conservatives," and are now assuming the title of "traditionalists" (even though we are fundamentally altering the doctrinal legacy of Methodism) should be allowed to go too.

Their reasoning was absurd, of course, and any disaffiliating pastor's attempt to use ¶2553 was sure to be refused by the bishops. Except, they didn't. The Council of Bishops, as divided as the church itself, unable to agree upon a unified episcopal response to the campaign for "disaffiliation" being waged by conservatives, folded. Bishops should have said to conservative would-be disaffiliates, "You're *not* unhappy with our church's stand against gays? Then why are you taking my time talking about ¶2553? Doesn't apply to your forebodings about the issue that you claim to be not your only issue."

However, some bishops, notably in the Southeast and parts of Texas, cowered before separationist threats (or, like Bishops Jones and Lowry, opportunistically jumped on board with the disaffiliates) and allowed traditionalists to use ¶2553 as a path out, muttering, "Good riddance."

In fact, ¶2553 gave a "limited right" to "disaffiliate," but it bore an expiration date, December 31, 2023. As we shall see, at Buncombe Street, aspiring lay disaffiliators (a word?) eagerly began feverish, though clandestine work lest ¶2553 expire, discovering allies, intimidating clergy, and strategizing to pressure their congregation to vote their way out of The UMC. An unprecedented barrage of media hype from the WCA, then the GMC aided by the Institute of Religion and Democracy (IRD) assaulted Methodism. Law firms like Detroit-based Dalton & Tomich, Louisiana's Lloyd Lunceford, Esq., and a stampede of others offered their services. Disaffiliates at Buncombe Street would eventually hire a right-wing firm from Florida, quickly finding the fifty-thousand-dollar retainer fee among their ranks. From the first, disaffiliates made schism a legal matter, lawyering up, suing bishops, and threatening litigation, even though no United Methodist threatened to sue them. Lawyers packed YouTube with offers to help disaffiliates sue their way out of The UMC. First consultation free. Intimidated bishops trembled before the onslaught of lawyers.

A couple of bishops, including Bishop Holston of South Carolina, went against the advice of UMC counsel, as well as their episcopal colleagues and, while borrowing some of the voting procedures and deadlines from the *Discipline*'s ¶2553, seized upon ¶2549: rules for what to do when a church dies. Not only is ¶2549 irrelevant to those who wish to leave The UMC because of disagreements over UMC doctrine and policy, but it is also open-ended: No expiration date.

An aside: The elimination of the trust clause is the single doctrinal revision of the UMC made by the GMC. They'll have to keep connected solely through argument and persuasion. That's not only unprecedented in Methodism but tough in a breakaway denomination composed of people who formed a new church out of their fear of denominational dispute and spirited exhortation. Having once successfully swiped a congregation from a denomination, what's to keep a church, at the first whiff of disagreement, from sticking it to the GMC? Be suspicious of any marriage that begins by a couple saying upfront that, while they're very much in love, someone richer or better looking might come along, so they'd rather not sign anything that might limit their options.

Unknown to most Buncombe Streeters, emerging influencers like lay leaders Krista Bannister and Janice Holliday were not waiting for national denominational events to trickle down to Greenville. Under the radar, they began hosting meetings in their homes, carefully vetting invitees, plotting for a new, revised, and purified Buncombe Street.

Nobody was so boorish as to bring up Paul: "We reject secrecy and shameful actions. We don't use deception, and we don't tamper with God's word. Instead, we commend ourselves to everyone's conscience in the sight of God by the public announcement of the truth" (2 Cor 4:2).

Numerous people reported to me how, in these living room meetings, documentation (boilerplate provided by the WCA and the IRD) was presented that revealed shocking secrets: heresy and apostasy throughout Methodism, drag queens and worse running rampant all over The UMC. We're telling you secrets that our pastors and their denominational bosses don't want you to know. The Resurrection? They don't believe it. And you can say goodbye to the Apostles' Creed. Virgin birth too. Your next pastor could be gay. Don't say you weren't warned.

Krista and her husband, Jim, even attended a WCA national briefing and training session in Indianapolis. What they learned there would equip them to convince, in just a few months, Buncombe Streeters that somehow the denomination's agonies on display at Saint Louis spelled life or death for a congregation in Greenville.

My friend John Redmond recalls being invited to the Bannisters' in March 2022 where, after attempting to gauge John's openness to the idea of separation, they announced that they were moving full steam to put Buncombe Street at the head of the line of disaffiliating congregations. John urged them to wait and see what happens at the upcoming General Conference. His appeal for patience and reserve was rejected; John never got another invitation to the Bannisters'.

By the next month, an unidentified group, "Friends to Preserve Buncombe Street," began a professionally designed email campaign (using the church's email list without authorization), demanding a congregational petition to vote on disaffiliation. Who slipped the confidential email list to the Friends? Nobody knows.

Within a couple of weeks, the "Friends," still unidentified, announced that more than four hundred people had signed a petition to disaffiliate from The United Methodist Church, even though some of the signatories told me that they thought they were simply expressing interest in hearing more about the issues, not signing on to split the church.

To the chagrin of many, the district superintendent, Jim Dennis, received the petition and said he would discuss it with the bishop. On June 27, 2022, retired businessmen Coleman Shouse and John Redmond met with Superintendent Dennis, telling him that "there were hundreds of people at Buncombe Street who were not happy about the slanted views being presented and the unfair ways in which this entire process was unfolding." Dennis thanked them for their interest.

While I like to think that my efforts over the past couple of years in the denominational debate (*Don't Look Back*) saved lots of UM churches from schism, as you shall see, I failed to save the church that saved me.

Pastoral Cares

My last summer of life in Greenville, 1964, I piled all my treasures in one suitcase and set sail for the exotic wonders of Wofford College. Thirty miles away. The previous fall, Wofford was the first private college in South Carolina to racially integrate. Though I heard a number of grownups at Buncombe Street grumble, "Wofford has given in to the gov'ment," and lament, "I tell you, Miss Diggs, the Methodist Church has gone liberal," I wrote a letter to the *South Carolina Methodist Advocate* saying I was proud to be a freshman, pleased to have a scholarship, grateful that Wofford was doing what's right, ashamed of those Methodist churches that were withholding funds from Wofford.

"Ruffled a few feathers with your letter," joshed our pastor, Dr. Robert N. Dubose, in the hallway after service. I hoped he was secretly proud of me.

That summer, South Carolina's Bishop Paul Hardin (nicknamed "The Golden Tongue" during his student days at Wofford) preached at Buncombe Street. (Just five years before, when Bishop Hardin was pastor of First Methodist, Birmingham, he had been one of the recipients of Martin Luther King Jr.'s historic "Letter from Birmingham Jail." None of us had heard of King's letter.)

Slouching sullenly in the pew next to my mother, I listened to the bishop's sermon, sort of. Eagerly bound for being unbound in college, having decided that being a Christian required a lobotomy, I remember only one story from Bishop Hardin's sermon.

After a bit of wandering, bragging that his Volkswagen Beetle could outrace "even Buicks," mouthing a few vague generalities about love of neighbor, especially people who work in grocery stores and who empty trash, the bishop concluded with this story:

"Back during my courting days, while I was a theology student at Candler, I was calling on a young lady who lived a couple of miles from campus in Decatur. How I dreaded that long walk back to Emory on Sunday nights when I had lingered too long after supper!

"Back in those days there were streetlights only as far as the edge of town. That last few hundred yards back to campus were dark, so dark, walking alone in somebody else's town.

"So I drew a deep breath and stepped into the darkness, picking up my pace, trying not to stumble. I became aware of steps behind me. Heavy steps. I looked back over my shoulder. In the night, I made out the shadow of a huge, giant of a man coming up behind me.

"A black man.

"I walked faster. His steps quickened. I picked up speed, almost running, even though I couldn't see for sure where I was going. Looking back over my shoulder in terror I saw that he was gaining on me. I stumbled and fell! When I hit the ground I fumbled wildly for a stick, a rock, anything with which to defend myself.

"My pursuer's body loomed over me now. He looked down upon me . . . smiling. Even in the dark, I could see his great smile as he reached down and helped me up. 'You are 'bout the fastest man I ever saw,' my good Samaritan said as he lifted me off the ground. 'I been trying to catch up with you for the longest time. It's so dark, too dark to be walking by yourself. Better for the both of us if we walk together. Right?"

Bishop Hardin paused for full rhetorical affect, and then pronounced, slowly, "We've got lots of tensions among us. Some of you are upset that the world is changing. Maybe it's a good time to remember that the dark is so dark, too dark to walk it alone. Jesus has given us one another for the long way home. Let's walk together. In Jesus's name. Together. Amen."

When I told Dr. Dubose that I enjoyed hearing Bishop Hardin, he confided, "Good. I only invited him because I'm hoping to shut up some of the know-it-alls around here who are in a tizzy that the bishop is pressuring us to merge the Black and the white conferences."

Considered at this distance, I doubt that you are impressed by the bishop's too veiled reference to racial justice in this Buncombe Street sermon from sixty years ago. Looking back, I know he ought to have said more and said it differently. Still, it's one of the few moments I can remember anybody saying anything about the racial reckoning that was shaking the earth under Buncombe Street, a rare instance of an episcopal leader (and our pastor as well), speaking up and attempting to lead a congregation where God surely wanted us to go.

"I don't trust that bishop," an oldster grumbled in the parking lot that Sunday. Eight years later, my first year in ministry, Paul Hardin would lead the Black and white South Carolina conferences to merger, forced to do so by The United Methodist Church and its trust clause. I'm fairly sure that conference delegates from Buncombe Street didn't think much of that move and voted against it.

This I recall to suggest to you that a group of people at Buncombe Street being unhappy with the larger church and its bishops is nothing new. While there were people who grumbled about pressure being put upon us by the denomination and its hierarchy back then, I give thanks to God there was no secretive small group at Buncombe Street to sever us from the church that, even in a bumbling way, told us some truth about our sin and helped us to begin to repent. Where would I be, in my own relationship to Christ, if Bishop Hardin had allowed us to disaffiliate before The United Methodist Church had time to tell me the truth?

Since Noah and the ark, Buncombe Street enjoyed thinking of ourselves as having the best paid (except for an upstart faux, proto-mega Methodist church in the Lowcountry), most educated (but not eggheads), sophisticated (still, with the common touch), genteel (but unpretentious) preachers money could buy. All with the bishop's approval, of course.

Just about everyone I have interviewed in the Buncombe Street dispute agrees: there's no way to understand what happened there without knowing that the congregation experienced a two-decade lacuna of ministerial leadership. Buncombe Street may have been the second-largest United Methodist church in South Carolina, an annual contributor of over $400,000 to the annual conference (4 percent of the conference budget) but, judging from the series of short-term senior pastor appointments and haphazard staff hires, securing strong, Wesleyan ministerial leadership for Buncombe Street was a low priority for the bishop and cabinet.

I say this knowing the irony of my criticism. As bishop in Alabama, I also sometimes took strong churches for granted, assuming they could handle just about any pastor I sent their way. It's a peculiar episcopal blindness—we focus on problem churches while inadvertently creating problems in healthy ones. *Mea culpa.*

An Alabama Methodist farmer was candid about his doubts of my episcopal competence in handling ministerial succession in his little congregation. "Bishop, things are going so good at our church, we're scared that you are going to drop some dud on us, thinking nobody can mess us up. Well, we ain't as healthy as we look."

Did a succession of bishops erroneously think that Buncombe Street was so placid and well-fixed that the quality of ministerial appointment didn't matter?

Years ago, I asked my mentor, veteran church observer Bob Wilson, "Why, in city after city, the Presbyterians, Baptists, Lutherans, and even the Episcopalians succeed at having active, large urban congregations but Methodists don't?"

With typical bluntness, Bob replied, "Bishops are toxic to large, downtown Methodist churches. Behind every Methodist urban church that's died, there is a series of bad clergy appointment decisions by a bishop."

As a sometime bishop in Alabama, I know the huge expectations placed on bishops. Every appointment involves weighing competing goods—congregational stability versus clergy career aspirations, local church preferences versus conference-wide needs, the mission of a congregation, and the availability of competent clergy to lead that particular church's mission. And yet Wilson's tough judgment contains enough truth to make this former bishop wince. Looking back at what happened at my home church, I see how questionable episcopal decisions, even if well intentioned, can weaken a congregation's gratitude for and connection to Methodism.

When a bishop and cabinet fail to prioritize and recognize the unique pastoral leadership challenges presented by large, urban congregations, they find that these churches are more fragile than they may outwardly appear.

United Methodists often lament the plight of our small, rural congregations. Most of their concerns are unjustified. Though these churches are small, they are tough and resilient. When Bob Wilson and I researched and wrote our *Preaching and Worship in the Small Church*, we found that, because their members are more engaged and steadfast than those in larger churches, changes in clergy leadership tend to have less impact on small churches than on large congregations.

United Methodism's most threatened and vulnerable congregations, judged by the statistics on membership, attendance, and giving, are churches that, just twenty years ago, boasted over a thousand members. The Buncombe Streets of Methodism are a dying breed and the key factor is appropriate fit of senior pastoral leadership. Large United Methodist congregations often feel they need the denomination less than the denomination needs them. If they ever think about their bishop, it's for only one reason: the bishop has sole responsibility for selecting their clergy. As they see it, if a bishop fails to appoint them the pastor they think they must have to survive, the bishop has flopped at everything.

When I became bishop in Alabama, assigned the overwhelming task of managing a complex ecclesiastical organization (over eight hundred churches), I convinced a recently retired corporate executive to be my "Bishop's Management Coach." Layman Bill Hamer taught me management skills, critiqued my leadership, shadowed me at meetings, and gave me guidance in my day-to-day episcopal oversight of pastors and congregations. As I recounted in my book *Bishop*, I would frequently ask Bill to study congregations of concern, assessing them and advising me and the cabinet on pastoral appointments and transitions.

"I've been at the top of a multimillion-dollar company, taught management and administration in two different colleges," Bill loved to say, "but I tell you, your pastors who are effectively leading larger congregations, though few and far between, are the most remarkable leaders I've encountered."

The complexity of life in a big, voluntary, loosely connected organization is a leadership challenge for which no seminaries prepare preachers. In The United Methodist Church, no pastor can dismiss any church member and, while pastors are expected to supervise church staff, they have no direct responsibility to pay, hire, or fire any of the staff under their supervision. Although it's absurd, most bishops do not even give the senior pastors of large churches the opportunity to approve of the appointment of the associate and assistant pastors whom bishops assign to their church staffs.

As is the case with all pastors, senior pastors of larger congregations are totally dependent upon the quality of their personal influence, trust, persuasion, and relationship with staff and church members in order to get anything done. Yet the size, anonymity, and diversity of a large congregation make that hard.

Most pastors cut their teeth leading small congregations where they are able to foster personal, hands-on connections with the few decision-makers, gatekeepers, and power brokers within the congregation. The more conscientious and hard-working a pastor, the more opportunities to build deep relationships and gain more influence over the identity and direction of a small congregation.

Not so in larger churches. In all my family's years at Buncombe Street, we never had a member of the church staff visit in our home. "If we had wanted personal attention from the pastor, we would have joined a smaller church," my mother would say, defensively. We would have never been connected with a pastor were it not for my being an officer of the Methodist Youth Fellowship. In large churches there are just too many members for a pastor to utilize one-on-one personal connections with individuals that undergird the pastor's leadership of the congregation. Any pastor who is assigned to a large congregation must therefore have the personality and acquire appropriate management and leadership skills to guide a church of this size, or failure is inevitable.

In a denomination where the average attendance in the typical United Methodist church is under fifty, where over 80 percent of our congregations have under two hundred members, pastors who have large-church experience are few and it is all too easy for bishops and their cabinets unintentionally to neglect their few larger churches. To be sure, their inattention makes no sense: big congregations pay the lion's share of the cost of the annual conference and the general church (to say nothing of the bishop's salary). Ascending to their pulpits is the heart's desire for the most talented clergy in the conference; and they have a disproportionately large number of Methodists worshipping Jesus on any given Sunday.

When I met with the Clergywomen's Caucus in Alabama, of all the things they could have asked of me, their chief demand was "You need to appoint more women to our biggest churches."

Larger congregations like Buncombe Street are the vocational goal of our most talented and able clergy and ought to receive the appointive priority they deserve.

In North Alabama, twelve of our largest congregations paid one-third of our conference budget. After I invited those pastors to lunch, I thanked them for their leadership and their congregations' money and then said, "It has occurred to me that the changes I'm working on for the conference and the innovations that must be ventured, all of you have already accomplished in your churches. Teach me how." Most of them reported that this was the first conversation they had ever had with a bishop, even though their churches were paying the largest share of my salary.

By the way: Many of those large churches represented at that luncheon in Birmingham are now affiliated with the Global Methodist Church.

After nearly an hour of conversation and debate in our cabinet over the appointment of a pastor to a church, I mused, "We began today by appointing a pastor to a church with an average attendance of five hundred (which means it's in the top twenty-five of our eight hundred congregations). Our deliberation took fifteen minutes. We just spent the better part of an hour fussing over the chronic problems of a pastor to a congregation with an attendance of barely 100. What's wrong with this picture?"

One more. After careful study (with Bill Hamer's help) of a once-flourishing urban congregation, I appointed a thirty-year-old to the position of senior pastor, a young man with unusual gifts and superb preparation. It proved to be one of my most controversial moves. "Too big a jump," said some envious older pastors. "He got a twelve thousand dollar increase in salary," griped other critics. There was no mention of the past leadership failures that had contributed to the decline of this church, nor any concern for the specific mission needs of this particular congregation.

My retort: "Whenever a pastor is appointed to a congregation, particularly to a large congregation in need, based upon factors other than the specific requirements to lead the mission of that congregation, the Methodist appointive system is degraded and Wesley's wonderful, adaptive church-as-mission polity is betrayed." That pastor is still leading that congregation over a decade later.

"I fear you have become distracted by your desire for affirmation by your fellow clergy," warned coach Bill Hamer when I told him that—against his advice, and the self-assessment of the lay leadership of the congregation—I was going to appoint a pastor to a historic downtown church because "he has long dreamed of serving that congregation and he has been a wonderful district superintendent."

In six months, attendance dropped 10 percent. We were forced to move the pastor mid-year. We followed him with a talented young woman who had a great six-year run as senior pastor.

———

After a succession of pastoral appointments, some at Buncombe Street concluded that the various bishops had disregarded the unique mission needs and personality of this large, urban congregation. In the seventeen years between 1998 and 2015, Buncombe Street cycled through a succession of senior pastors. While each brought gifts to the congregation, the cumulative effect of these short tenures was erosion of stable pastoral leadership. The congregation learned to function with minimal dependence on pastoral direction—a lack that would be the crucial factor when lay leaders later moved to separate from the denomination.

In 1997 former Rhodes Scholar Bob Stillwell was appointed to Buncombe Street. People still grieved the death of the adored Bill Reid. Bob told me that he stood up to some of the powerful old-timers and paid a price. There were complaints that Bob's preaching was "too intellectual." He was told he ought to "tell more stories" in his sermons. In a scant three years the bishop moved Bob.

Jerry Temple followed in 2007. Some of the laity were concerned that this was "too big a jump" and that Jerry—a kind, sweet-spirited, humble, evangelical of a pastor—wasn't up to the expectations of well-to-do, downtown, sophisticated Buncombe Street. Jerry's training had been at conservative Asbury Seminary; Buncombe Street's pastors had always come from Duke or Emory. Jerry's previous appointment was Mauldin UMC (an unpretentious suburb of Greenville) that seemed to some an unwarranted elevation to big Buncombe Street.

Most people liked Jerry. Some complained that his sermons were simplistic, laced with personal stories about family and personal tribulation. But Jerry took administration seriously, which was something the church hadn't had in a while, attempting to empower laity to lead. "Old Jerry believed laity always know best and the senior minister's job was to implement whatever the laity want," smirked one old-timer—then adding, "Some would say that Jerry led, only from behind."

Jerry, a committed evangelical, noted the need for the church to attract new, younger members. However, "the new people who joined Buncombe Street tended to lack knowledge of or experience with Methodism," recalled one lay leader.

Despite Jerry's conscientious efforts, the perception was that the congregation was drifting. For the first time in its history, Buncombe Street hired staff without denominational vetting or episcopal oversight. In 2001, sometime Baptist hoping to become a Methodist deacon Grover Putnam volunteered to work in the church's day care center. When an opening came in the staff, Grover was eager to take on young adult ministry. Didn't work out. Grover was transferred to care of the aging and homebound. Renowned for his note-writing, and universally beloved, Grover was never too Methodist. He turned in his deacon's credentials by 2023, successfully dodging Methodism's clergy vetting system.

Amid senior pastor comings and goings, Grover gained influence as the one continuing member of the church staff. Grover's wife, Debbie, also led through her "loudly conservative" (as more than one person described them) Facebook posts. One senior pastor asked Grover to tell Debbie to take down some of her more inflammatory Facebook apocalyptic rants against liberals.

While writing this book, I saw that Debbie is now leading a women's Tuesday Bible study on when and where Jesus will pull the plug and the world will end. Matthew 24:36 notwithstanding.

Then, in 2015, at the recommendation of District Superintendent George Howle, young Justin Gilreath was selected as associate pastor at Buncombe Street. Justin's sole ministerial experience, since his graduation from Duke Divinity School, was as pastor of a rural UMC in Anderson County. Perhaps George and the bishop thought that at Buncombe Street young Justin would receive supervision and guidance by more experienced senior clergy.

Justin was a local pastor, a designation generally used for those laity who, called to ministry in later life, have not had the opportunity for college and seminary. This was the first time in history that a lowly local pastor had been appointed as a leader of grand Buncombe Street, a signal to some that the church was not high on the bishop's list of priorities.

Justin's defenders were quick to add that his grandfather, physician Pat Meakin, and grandmother, Dot, had been members of Buncombe Street. Justin even attended Buncombe Street awhile as a child, brought by the Meakins. In sermons, Justin recounted fond memories of church at Buncombe Street followed by lunch at the Greenville Country Club. He was a native son, sort of.

Justin grew up under the preaching of a Baptist who had a long run as a lay preacher at Jackson Grove UMC, whose Facebook page says, "We are a small, country church located between Travelers Rest & Greer, SC." (Jackson's main claim was to be the home church of William Preston

Few, first president of Duke.) Justin jokingly described in a sermon his time at Duke Divinity as the "three most miserable years of my life" during which he constantly had to "defend my faith." "I didn't agree with a lot that they tried to teach me" at Duke "cemetery."

While serving at his previous appointment at Piedmont, Justin went to Erskine Seminary for his doctor of ministry degree (just after the University Senate dropped conservative, Associate Reformed Presbyterian Erskine from the list of approved seminaries to prepare United Methodist pastors).

Justin lived with his young family on the family's farm outside of Travelers Rest, thirty minutes from Buncombe Street. That farm, along with its pickup truck (pistol in the glove compartment in case "somebody tries to mess with me"), dog, and feed trough, would figure prominently in Justin's career trajectory and in his sermons. When questioned by the Pastor-Staff Relations Committee about his ordination status, he assured them he would soon seek elders' orders, reminding them of his Duke MDiv and Erskine DMin.

However, once Justin was ensconced at Buncombe Street, receiving acclamation for his sermons at the contemporary service, he declared that he wouldn't seek ordination in The UMC. Justin had made a vow to his daddy that he would be at the farm every Friday.

Because Justin had been hired at Buncombe Street without the bishop or district superintendent having heard him preach or teach, his decision not to enter the process of candidacy for ordination was, for some with whom I talked, the earliest warning that Justin had misgivings about United Methodism. Others said, "Who cares if Justin doesn't want to be uprooted from his family's farm by the whims of a bishop?" We've at last gotten ourselves (without the aid of any bishop, thank you) an ambitious, gifted young preacher who is grateful to be here.

To those who expressed concern about a non-vetted, untested, uncredentialed young pastor being installed at Buncombe Street, the response was, "Look what the vetting, testing, and credentialing by the S. C. Conference Board of Ordained Ministry has gotten us in the last decade." Enough said.

In 2016, when the bishop moved Jerry Temple, the new pastor, Bob Howell (who loathed contemporary worship) totally turned the contemporary worship service over to Justin. Down at Summerville UMC for nearly two decades, Bob had made it one of the largest churches in the conference. Having begun his career as assistant minister at Buncombe Street years before under Bryan Crenshaw, Bob dreamed of returning as senior pastor. Welcome back, Bob.

The church initially profited from Bob's energetic administration. Problems with evangelism, fundraising, and facilities were addressed. The contemporary service was renamed "The Table." A big investment updated the makeshift situation at the gym into a well-appointed, techno wonder auditorium for the service where attendance was growing steadily, showing congregational enthusiasm for Justin's full-time focus on preaching.

One frequent visitor told me that the main thing that impressed newcomers was the contrast between Bob's service in the sanctuary, "where it was hard to hear the preacher, and the sermon sounded like it was just thrown together," with Justin's "well planned contemporary service where the lighting, sound, and timing were perfect and the sermon was easy to understand and energetically, enthusiastically delivered."

The Table's ascendancy over the stuffy traditional service, the division of the congregation into one service that belonged to now-ailing Bob and the other to young, dynamic Justin was ironic. Justin's 2010, 59,000-word Erskine DMin dissertation, "Enhancing Community Development and Relationships Between Two Worship Services: A Study of First Corinthians," dealt with the unhealthy split in Justin's little Piedmont church caused by having two competing worship services, traditional and contemporary. Justin was now doing at Buncombe Street what he said Paul disapproved of in Corinth.

Amid the comings and goings of less than enthusiastically received senior pastors, now and then there was talk about the upcoming 2020 General Conference, but only among the few who had heard of General Conference. "You can mark my word," someone said to somebody during a Bible study, "they'll let Methodist ministers perform same sex-marriages!"

Unknown to the senior pastor, a few influential (but as yet unnamed) members were now in active contact with the Wesleyan Covenant Association and the Institute of Religion and Democracy, receiving and discreetly circulating their onslaughts that warned of the Armageddon sure to come at the 2020 General Conference. Bob Howell ordered the Buncombe Street staff to say nothing to anyone about possible denominational conflict. Bob followed a time-honored pastoral principle: know nothing, say nothing, confirm nothing; maybe it will go away.

The 2016 General Conference had created a Way Forward Committee which met for a year and accomplished little. As best I can tell, the radically new, completely inappropriate, euphemistic term "disaffiliate" was coined in the Way Forward debacle.

Again, the BSUMC staff was ordered to say nothing.

———————

Sometime in 2017, dwindling Trinity United Methodist Church on Augusta Road in south Greenville was told by the Greenville DS that they would die a slow, agonizing death if they weren't taken over by another UM church. Bob Howell saw this as an opportunity for Greenville's first ever UMC "satellite" arrangement. Bob even had someone in mind to serve Trinity, Ben Burt. By 2018, Buncombe Street and Trinity were strong-armed by Bob into becoming two congregations, one church. Sort of. More or less.

Years of tensions and wrangling between Trinity and Buncombe Street ensued. Too many questions left unanswered, blurred lines of accountability and responsibility, differing congregational cultures, and constant bickering over money. Both congregations blamed Bob for the haphazard way the two were joined. Attendance slipped to fewer than a hundred at Trinity. Big Buncombe Street Daycare Center unwillingly took over Trinity's small, equally unwilling, day care center. Necessary building maintenance was left undone. Trinity's deed was offered, but never accepted or signed by Buncombe Street, though some at Buncombe Street thought they had. Promises were made and broken. I've got pages of meeting minutes, unsigned agreements, angry charges and counthercharges, if you want to see them.

The complicated relationship with the Trinity campus exemplified Buncombe Street's growing disconnect from Methodist connectionalism. What should have been a story of Methodist churches supporting each other in mission became instead another example of institutional ties fraying. The mishandled merger created wounds that would later be a factor in the disaffiliation story.

Personally, I had nearly as close a connection with Trinity as I had with Buncombe Street. Trinity was served by my father-in-law, the fabled Carl Parker, back in the 1960s when Patsy and I were in high school. Sometimes we dated to the MYF meetings at Trinity. Many Saturdays we sat in the Trinity parking lot (the Parkers' parsonage was next door). Talking. I can still see Reverend Parker, standing on the back stoop of the parsonage, 11:00, Saturday night, bellowing into the darkened lot, "You two come on inside to the living room. You can do in here whatever you're doing out there. I've got to preach tomorrow!"

What I remember most gratefully about Trinity UMC is its inadequately lit parking lot.

———

Then on Halloween night 2019, as the popular Buncombe Street Church administrator gave out candy to trick-or-treaters, he slipped and fell down his front steps. He died November 7, 2019. Prior to the funeral, it was discovered he and the even more popular BSUMC music director were having an affair. She was fired. His funeral was awkward. The pain of it all was made worse by rumors that Jerry Temple had ordered them to cease their affair, but was disregarded. Then somebody said that Bob Howell knew, or should have known, about their misbehavior but didn't really follow through. In a tense January meeting with the bishop, Bob abruptly resigned and retired.

The bishop assigned retired, kindly Mike Guffee as caretaker interim to fill out the year. Justin continued to grow The Table and to attract grateful listeners.

———

In January 2020, far away from Greenville, an unlikely, small but diverse group of UMC conflict-weary bishops, LBGTQ advocates, right-wing UMC haters, conservative and liberal agitators, naive peacemakers, appeasers, and self-appointed leaders issued a protocol of reconciliation, mediated by a Jewish attorney, that offered a proposal for congregations to leave The UMC. The trust clause be damned.

The bishops saw themselves as peacemakers, appeasers who were working for a friendly divorce settlement whereby The UMC could at least keep a couple of the kids, grandmother's coffee table, and the dog. Everybody else was working for as big a slice of the United Methodist pie as they could get, at as low a price as possible.

"You don't know what this WCA crowd is like," said one bishop when I asked why on earth he had become involved with the protocol debacle. "We have got to reach some accommodation with them or they will tie up the church in court with lawsuits for the rest of eternity. If the price of their going quietly is a few hundred congregations and a cash settlement for other assets, I say let's pay, let them go wherever they can be happy, and get on with being the church." (Dumb me. Having been named in a dozen lawsuits when I was bishop, I had assumed that having to defend the church in court was just part of a bishop's job.)

The protocol of reconciliation fiasco was all done outside of church legislative channels and anything they came up with would need to be approved by the upcoming General Conference. When COVID killed the planned General Conference, church-wide disapproval and yawns killed the protocol. Once the bishops involved in the protocol were stunned by blowback from the church at large, they jumped ship and repudiated their participation in the IRD/WCA publicity stunt. The conservatives denounced the ex-protocol bishops as traitors and cowards. See you at General Conference.

The protocol of reconciliation's only accomplishment was in legitimizing a couple of marginal, minuscule agitation groups of the right and of the left, giving credence to the bogus notion of "disaffiliation," and building the self-confidence of those who now, more than ever, wanted to tear apart The UMC. Who's afraid of the big bad trust clause now?

Amid this uncertain, contentious denominational climate, in July 2020, Brian Gilmer was appointed senior pastor, moved from a small-town church nearby, and deacon Karen Jones was appointed as an associate to BSUMC, just in time for COVID. Justin Gilreath, you will recall, had been at Buncombe Street since 2015, Grover Putnam longer. Both had profited from the short-term senior pastor appointments of the preceding years. "As far as I was concerned, Justin was the real chief preacher at our church," said one person who would become a leader of the disaffiliates. "Only the bishop thought Brian belonged there."

Brian remembered that District Superintendent Jim Dennis had urged, "Help them become United Methodist again. You have a lot of business leaders, lawyers, Type A's. They don't like to be told what to do. Help them get back on track and help them understand United Methodism." This was an insufficient warning for what Brian actually confronted.

"There were three churches, not one," recalled Brian, "traditional, The Table, and the Trinity campus. The adoption of Trinity had been handled poorly so it lacked direction." ("Abduction" rather than adoption is the way some Trinity leaders described it.)

I heard many, including former pastors, say, "Buncombe Street is really two congregations: the early, contemporary service, The Table, and the eleven o'clock traditional service. Then there's that little group over at Trinity." From multiple conversations, I'd say Buncombe Street was more nearly a dozen "congregations": the two worship services, a secretive group of disaffiliates, the "My-family-has-been-here-for-six-generations" old guard, adult Sunday school groups, the youth, the basketball crowd, Grover's home-bound folks, those who regularly attend, people who hardly ever attend (majority of those on the roll, I'd say), the struggling few at Trinity. I could go on. As Lyle Schaller told me when I was pastor at Duke University Chapel, "There's no such thing as a large church. There are only sets of small congregations that convene in a large building."

Brian tried to share the various services among the staff, in order to create more unity. "My vision is that we need to be on same team," he told them.

"But then there was the pandemic. We got there in July; staff were sent home in March and didn't go back in person until October 2020! We had a Reopen Task Force that was very cautious about the pandemic and lots of people were upset over how we handled it," said Brian. No staff meetings or accountability, no church gatherings, online worship, anti-maskers fuming, and, amid it all, a perceived vacuum of leadership.

"Looking back on Brian's first year, nobody was working for Buncombe Street except the disaffiliates who were busy, very busy," said one lay leader who was ousted by the disaffiliation vote.

The contemporary service (The Table) had grown under Justin's preaching; Brian was saddled with the 11:00 o'clock, traditional. Those attending The Table were younger; many had little institutional knowledge of Buncombe Street United Methodist Church or Wesleyanism. All adored Justin.

Brian readily admits that he was ill suited to deal with a large, rambling, COVID-contentious congregation. The bishop advised all South Carolina pastors to be "neutral" and "objective" if the subject of disaffiliation came up; the less said, the better. Brian therefore declined to take sides. This middle-of-the-road silence, far from promoting a big-tent mood in the congregation or turning down the temperature, infuriated the separatists, and disappointed those who wished to stay UMC. With no one to counter the WCA's barrage of misinformation, Krista Bannister's list of unhappiness with The UMC was growing: the bishop's poor handling of Buncombe Street's pastoral assignments, the magnitude of the congregation's financial apportionments from The UMC, General Conference's sexual policies, lax biblical interpretation, alleged abandonment of belief in God in the seminaries, and rumored lack of commitment to the creeds by those who should know better.

In my Introduction to Ordained Leadership class at Duke I say, "Leadership is only needed if an organization needs to go somewhere." Leadership isn't optional for a church because of the demanding mission of Jesus Christ. From the first, someone had to step up and take responsibility for leading Jesus's people in the direction Jesus demanded that they go. An unidentified, but growing group felt Buncombe Street needed to go away from The UMC and if the clergy wouldn't step up and lead, they would. And lead they did.

Into the perceived vacuum stepped a small group of committed, some say "fanatical," I say confused but competent and heavily coached, well-organized and financed, determined lay leaders. Their way was paved by the silence of a senior pastor, a district superintendent, and a bishop who refused (or were unsuited) to be the debaters, defenders, or advocates The UMC paid them to be.

The size of the congregation was in the disaffiliates' favor. Even regular attenders didn't know what was going on, an understandable condition with the clergy's silence. Social media was quick to fill the information void with verbiage handed to them by the WCA.

While senior pastors came and went, this churn of ministerial leadership meant that institutional memory and Methodist identity increasingly resided with lay leaders rather than clergy—a shift that would prove significant when questions of denominational loyalty arose.

Years ago, fellow Wofford grad Wade Clark Roof, in a study of North Carolina Episcopalians, found that theological orthodoxy and church engagement go hand-in-hand. The theologically non-orthodox attend church less, contribute less money, and are less likely to engage in criticism or controversy in the congregation. The fierce commitment of conservatives makes up for what they lack in numbers, benefiting theological conservatives in power struggles with less engaged liberals in the congregation. Liberal, though-we-have-differences-we-can-all-get-along theology is no match for conservative, us-against-them crusaders. When it comes to a vote, those who feel called by God to dismantle and disrupt have an advantage; the majority of members (particularly in a large, low-commitment church like Buncombe Street) just want peacefully to be left alone.

Brian recalled that early on, Les and Bobby Pritchard, active lay leaders, came to his office "under pretense of getting to know me." They told Brian they were "concerned about the future of the church," and then went right to the point: "Where do you stand on same-sex marriage?"

At one of the first meetings with Staff-Parish Relations Committee, Brian was told, "You are the youngest senior pastor ever and the only one without a doctorate." He admitted that he was "deeply hurt."

Laymen Les Pritchard and Doug Stambaugh asked to meet with the pastoral staff, though Brian didn't know why. At this meeting, Les and Stacy Brandon (representing Doug, who had to be away on business) confronted each member of the staff, demanding that each declare where they were on the theological poles, "conservative or liberal." Enough of this wishy-washy silence, tell us what you really believe! (Stacy was destined to become the leader of The Way Forward committee.) Brian Gilmer reiterated that in order to serve all, and to promote open conversation in the congregation, he had asked the staff to avoid taking sides. The soon-to-be-out-in-the-open "disaffiliates" were furious.

"Krista Bannister got all her material straight from the WCA. She pushed the Global Methodist thing. The others just wanted to be independent. To me, it was not about human sexuality; it was power, money, and property. They didn't like being told what to do with their apportionment money and wanted to choose their pastor," Brian recalled.

Sometime around April 1 Brian got an email from Michael Helms, leader of the newly formed, separatist Friends to Preserve Buncombe Street, asking to meet with him. "We have a group who feel like we need to separate. We'd love you to be on our side but we'll move forward."

Brian told them, again, this time directly, "I'm not on your side." Before the day was over the Friends sent out their first public email, without anyone's permission, to all in the church data base.

Even though Brian had consistently told the staff, "We need to be a unified voice," and had asked staff to work together, Grover, David Stubbs, and Justin worked with the disaffiliates behind his back, according to a number of my sources at Open Hearts.

Brian sought but failed to receive much guidance or even encouragement from the annual conference and bishop. "I did feel like there were days trying to figure it out on my own. I was always asking questions [about Conference procedures for discernment] and they didn't have answers. Did seem, looking at other conferences, we were lagging behind."

"Justin let me know up front that, in spite of what he had told the church earlier, he had no intention to itinerate. . . . All he wanted to do was to work on his sermons. When I insisted that he take some committee and other responsibilities, he resisted."

At one point, frustrated Brian told Justin, "'Nobody can be senior pastor while you are here.' With the support of the separatists, Justin felt empowered, confident to say what he really thought and grow into who he really was."

In his August 7, 2022, sermon "What God Expects of Us," Justin preached at the Open Table service. Many remember his sermon as a watershed. Opening with "Are you worried about America right now? I am," he launched into "What's really worrying to me is that our country seems to be moving away from God. . . . Our country's almost given up on God altogether." "I feel like the church is under attack." "We need somebody to come and speak truth to America." Judgment. Just like Isaiah 1:10-17, "the lectionary text for today." (Lectionary, a gift from The UMC.)

> Hear the LORD's word, you leaders of Sodom.
>   Listen to our God's teaching,
>   people of Gomorrah!
>
> What should I think about all your sacrifices?
>   says the LORD.
> I'm fed up with entirely burned offerings of rams
>   and the fat of well-fed beasts.
>   I don't want the blood of bulls, lambs, and goats.
> When you come to appear before me,
>   who asked this from you,
>   this trampling of my temple's courts?
> Stop bringing worthless offerings.
>   Your incense repulses me.
> New moon, sabbath, and the calling of an assembly—
>   I can't stand wickedness with celebration! . . .
> Remove your ugly deeds from my sight.

> Put an end to such evil;
>> learn to do good.
> Seek justice:
>> help the oppressed;
>> defend the orphan;
>> plead for the widow.

Listen up, Sodom, I mean Greenville! The church no longer stands for the truth. Same-sex unions. Drag queens. Pastors persecuted, just for speaking the truth.

Then Justin mentioned, for the first time in public, that he'd heard criticism of "the Friends group." Emboldened by the recent "straw vote" (more about that in the next chapter) disobeying his senior pastor's directive, Justin openly lauded the disaffiliates: "Somebody's got to stand up for the truth in the culture today!"

Fresh from a week at the beach, Justin had had it with being silenced (by Brian). "Somebody needs to stand up and speak about what's going on in the church!" "My family is tired of it and we want to stand up for the truth."

Justin claimed that the Isaiah text is about the threatened punishment of Sodom and Gomorrah; surely he knows that "sodomy" is not Isaiah's subject. He tells his congregation that we can't just "go through the motions." We're not really loving God. Our heart has to be in the right place. "I love y'all but we're not really doing it right." Conveniently ignoring Isaiah's "Seek justice: help the oppressed," Justin jumped around with references to sin, judgment, confession, repentance, the Prodigal Son, Jesus as mediator, cited 1 John 4:20 on love [Careful. Wouldn't want anybody to think you were criticizing the "Friends" for lack of love.], pleaded for more praise and adoration in the congregation, criticized the American church for getting caught up in "social justice" and not really "saving souls." Who cares if Isaiah explicitly criticizes Israel's praise and adoration, not because Israel's worship is just going through the motions but because it's not combined with social justice?

Noting the upcoming congregational meetings related to disaffiliation, he said, "I've got to share with you what God has put on my heart." While Justin's sermon went in a number of different directions, people got the heartfelt message. The sermon is remembered by all as when Justin finally said what was really on his mind. The senior pastor recalled it as insubordination.

Then on October 30, 2022, a couple of hours before the culminating second vote, Justin came out. He says he wouldn't preach his personal opinions, just the pure word of God. However,

> Whenever a denomination strays from teaching the truth that has been taught by the church down to the ages, things can get messy. You have to decide what's important enough to divide over. . . . Sometimes there comes a time when you need to have a divorce. . . . What are your theological beliefs that you would literally die for? Separation has to be done in love, if it has to be done. Sometimes I've had to speak the truth to people, and it is hard to speak the truth, but necessary. . . . Jesus said there will be division. This is not a battle of progressive or conservative. It is a spiritual battle. All of us are broken. People have always fought in the church. I remind you today, not to hold too tightly on the building, however, you follow this. I have a lot invested in this building, third generation. But this building doesn't save you, the denomination, UMC or GMC doesn't save you. I pray that we walk away from this day loving one another. Even if this doesn't go the way you want it to today, walk away and love. Don't put your hope in a vote, put your hope in Jesus.
>
> I've been preaching in this church for eight years, and I think it would be irresponsible of me to walk away without saying these things, just teaching God's word. . . . We are going to have to decide if we're going to abide by the Scriptures or not. You will have to make your own decision about what you're going to do.

Here was Justin, not saying but saying, criticizing idolatry to the building before a vote that's mostly about the building, urging everyone to love, even while they're thereby voting some people out of fellowship, telling them that they're voting on whether to "abide by the Scriptures or not," even though Scripture isn't on the ballot. Jesus, hardly mentioned.

Although Justin makes much of 1 Corinthians 11 in his Erskine dissertation, he doesn't refer to it in a sermon, even in his sermon before the divisive vote.

"I hear that there are divisions among you, and I partly believe it. It's necessary that there are groups among you, to make it clear who is genuine. . . . Will I praise you? No, I don't praise you in this" (1 Cor 11:18-19, 22).

————————

After two turbulent, trying years of rancor; charges and counter-charges; two painful, laborious congregational votes (details to follow); and the departure of the senior pastor with Justin made his successor, Buncombe Street had disaffiliated and named itself an "independent Methodist church." Now senior pastor, one of Justin's first acts was to take it upon himself to ordain Janice and Grover.

It was November 10, 2024. At the freshly independent Buncombe Street, it was not the Twenty-Fifth Sunday after Pentecost, it was Veterans Day Sunday after the reelection of Donald Trump. At The Table, after some predictably sweet-sounding praise music led by Emily Lynch Cupelli, Janice called forward all active military, praised them for fighting so we could freely gather for worship, and blessed them with a prayer, adding that as Christians, we're "all soldiers."

Rather than taking a post-presidential election victory lap, Justin followed with a surprising, darkly bellicose sermon loosely derived from Ephesians 6. His opening salvo: "Y'all know we're in a war?" He said that his job as a pastor was "to teach people to fight." We're "in a battle with the devil. . . . I know what it's like to be attacked by an enemy." His father was recently hospitalized; wife, Jenny, had an unspecified illness; and Justin's own chronic illness has put him in unrelenting pain for which he had received no help. Not only that, last January, somebody sent Justin a package that contained a satanic plastic skull and pentagram. "We are under spiritual attack."

"We all have enemies."

Through eighteen years in ministry, Justin admitted, "I wasn't battle-ready," so now he felt obligated to prepare the new Buncombe Street for difficult days of combat. He said that he was now working to shift the culture of Buncombe Street, and "we as a church need to be more ready for war." Jesus was never mentioned in the somber sermon, though Justin included an extended quote from George W. Bush's speech to the nation after 9/11.

"Don't want to start a civil war in this church," he chuckled. "But we need to get our swords ready."

I'd like to think that, if I had heard a pastor under my episcopal care preach a sermon so dark and disjointed, I would have called and said, "Brother, I want you to take some time away while we sort out what's going on with your soul." Hearing what I took to be a cry for help, I wished Justin was still a United Methodist. I wanted to tell him that, though I could only imagine what it must be like to have a chronic, painful illness, I had sympathy for what it's like to have a big, sprawling, expectant, and demanding staff and congregation on your shoulders. I wanted to tell him that there's help for overburdened pastors, that Jesus Christ has fought and won the war with Satan so we don't have to.

I wanted to be his bishop. But I wasn't.

On the Friday night after delivering this sermon, Justin went to his pickup, took out his pistol, and turned it upon himself.

A year before Justin's tragic end, he had called a friend excitedly to report, "Well, it looks like, once we disaffiliate, they're gonna make me senior pastor." His friend pleaded, "Are you really sure you want this? You can't stand church administration. You're a preacher. You're sure that's what God wants you to be. Once they dump this job on you, you'll have all the weight of the whole church and a big staff on your back. There's a heap of difference between being a young, upstart associate who preaches Bible sermons at the contemporary service and being the guy in charge. You need to get you some help."

Of all the sadness that Buncombe Street church produced, suffered, and had to work through, the tragic loss of Justin had to be the saddest.

Declaration of Independence

How did Buncombe Street arrive at the sadness of November 2024? Let's reconstruct that story. Back in the spring of 2022, after meeting for months, quietly gathering comrades and getting the right sort of people positioned on church committees, the disaffiliates were at last emboldened to go public with their intention to lead the congregation out of the denomination.

Fred Suggs took time from his law practice of defending corporations against their workers to play a major role in the spread of disaffiliating (mis)information. Fred got his broadsides—gay preachers, drag queens, heretics, wasted money—from his buddy back in Montgomery, John Ed Mathison, renowned (notorious?) leader of the WCA, whom Fred had known before coming to South Carolina. Below is what Fred dropped upon his unsuspecting roundtable Sunday school class, in lieu of the Bible study he was supposed to be teaching, the first that many had heard of disaffiliation.

Sunday school opened with the rousing "Onward Christian Soldiers," with stress on verse 3, "We are not divided, all one body we, one in hope and doctrine, one in charity." Hope, maybe. Doctrine, we'll see. Charity, check back in a couple of months.

"Good morning. As I look around this room of friends and fellow Methodists, I recognize that there may be many different opinions," said Fred. "The Buncombe Street members are facing an extremely important decision about our future, and each of us must be well informed and prayerfully decide the path we believe we should take. I have carefully researched this issue and believe it is my duty to present it to you." [From the first, disaffiliates cast themselves as just presenting information for people prayerfully to consider.]

This talk today is meant to be partisan; someone else can present the other side.

I believe Buncombe Street should immediately begin the process of disaffiliating from the United Methodist Church.

I have arrived at this conclusion because of irreconcilable theological differences. [Immediately, the attempt to cast the dispute as theological.]

Not just one issue drives my decision. [?]

These issues include:

The authority of Scripture

The importance of salvation vs. social activism

The size of the church bureaucracy, its significant cost, and its bureaucratic incompetency. [Something I've been complaining about for years. Thanks, Fred.]

Buncombe Street's annual apportionment to the United Methodist Conference is about $420,000. [Wonderful testimony to the church's steadfast support for the denomination.]

Affiliating with another conference would cost much less because of reduced bureaucracy, approximately half as much. ["Another conference"? Where did you get those numbers?]

In a 2019 UMC survey [By whom, of whom?], the question was asked,

"Which should be the primary focus of the UMC?" 68% of self identified progressives picked "Advocating for social justice to transform the world." 70% of traditionalists picked "Saving souls for Jesus Christ." [What's a "progressive," and who's a "traditionalist"?]

On salvation, half of self-identified progressives believe "there are ways to salvation that do not involve Jesus." By contrast, 86% of traditionalists believe "The *only* way to salvation is through a relationship with Jesus." [Any of these salvation-denying progressives at Buncombe Street?]

38% of progressives believe "Jesus committed sins like other people."

Chicago UMC Bishop Joseph Sprague denied the full deity and resurrection of Jesus Christ as well as the reliability of the Gospel [of] John. [No disaffiliate ever criticized any United Methodist who lived in South Carolina or even within the whole Southeastern Jurisdiction of the UMC. The disaffiliates had to go at least a thousand miles from Buncombe Street to find a disagreeable Methodist.]

In 2017, Bishop Karen Oliveto warned not to "create an idol out of Jesus Christ" who had "his bigotries and prejudices."

The official United Methodist News touted a website by Pastor Martin Thielen, who opposes "faith in a God of supernatural invention."

The United Methodist Church was formed in 1968. [I was there!] Originally US membership was 11 million. Now it's only 6,268,310 in the US with 13 million worldwide.

While US membership has steadily declined over the past half century, membership in Africa and Asia is growing.

American Methodists have been divided over the issue of homosexuality for fifty years. Every four years the issue is fiercely debated at the quadrennial conference. Each time the progressives have lost.

Currently the United Methodist church's *Book of Discipline* labels homosexuality a sin, bars the ordination of noncelibate homosexuals, and prohibits the blessing of same-sex marriages.

The Book of Discipline says that "the practice of homosexuality is incompatible with Christian teachings."

The current *Book of Discipline* reflects Biblical teaching. [Which is?] The Bible says what it says. [Says what?] Several months ago, Don Cockrill went through a painstaking analysis of what the Bible says about homosexuality. Don concluded that the Bible is clear from the Old Testament to the New that practicing homosexuals are living in sin. Don concluded that to read the Scriptures any other way is disingenuous. [The Bible is anything but clear on this subject. That's why there's an argument.] One might say, even Don might say, that they don't care what the Bible says [Who's "they"? Never had anybody in the UMC say they "don't care what the Bible says."]; they prefer the current progressives' embrace of that lifestyle [?] as acceptable and conforming to the culture of the present world. Traditionalists say follow the Scripture.

While the *Book of Discipline*'s stance on homosexuality is traditional, it appears that a majority of General Conference delegates from the U.S. want to change it. The existing position is supported by a coalition of American traditionalists and delegates from overseas. [Turned out not to be so.]

So conservatives win the votes at General Conference every four years. But they have failed to take control [!] of the denomination's seminaries [Evidence?] or its bureaucratic structure who have reacted with defiance and organized resistance. ["Not just one issue drives" Fred's argument?]

The problem is that Methodist Bishops and various conferences have refused to follow the *Book of Discipliine* [sic] without consequences. [Not true.] The United Methodist Church does not have police [!] to enforce compliance with the *Book of Discipline.*

Self-avowed practicing homosexuals are being ordained for the ministry and same-sex marriages are being conducted. [In South Carolina?]

There is even a Queer Clergy Caucus, which shows that the issue is not isolated. (see handout)

In 2016 the church's Western Jurisdiction elected a gay San Francisco pastor, Karen Oliveto, as the first openly lesbian bishop in the United Methodist church. [True. And what has that to do with Buncombe Street?]

United Methodism now has its first drag queen certified as an ordination candidate in Illinois. [But never ordained.] When performing as a drag queen, Isaac Simmons, dressed as a woman, uses the stage name Ms. Penny Cost (note the disrespectful play on words). (see handout)

Simmons belongs to the UMC in Bloomington, Illinois. Hope IJMC promotes LGBTQIA+ causes and is a self described "leader in the resistance movement" against traditional sexual morality in the UMC.

This same Northern Illinois conference ordained transgender activist M. Barclay who self identifies as neither male nor female.

I am fed up with the flouting of church disciplines by some bishops, some clergy and the UMC bureaucracy.

This is not a "gay people are not welcome here" message. If a gay person wants to sit in the pew with the rest of us sinners that's ok, but they are not going to be ordained as ministers and they are not going to have same-sex weddings in any church that I belong to. [What gay Christian wouldn't warm to Fred's gracious invitation?]

Both camps are frustrated with the impasse.

Early in 2020 representatives of the traditionalist and the liberals negotiated the Protocol for Separation.

The Protocol allows for the creation of a new conservative denomination that would retain traditional teachings.

The Protocol allows individual congregations by majority vote (50% + 1) to withdraw without forfeiting their property. If approved, the new denomination would receive $25 M from the United Methodist Church.

Plans to vote on the Protocol were derailed by Covid-19. The General Conference initially set for May 2020 was postponed to the summer of 2021, then rescheduled for the fall, then in March of this year, pushed back to 2024. Allegedly because of Covid, third world representatives can't get vaccinated or get visas in order to travel here for the conference.

Conservatives think it was delayed again because liberals have changed their minds about the Protocol. The Conservatives believe that the reasons for the delay are a pretext. Conservatives say that other denominations are having their conferences on schedule, and that no real effort has previously been made to help third world delegates get vaccinated and obtain visas so they could attend the GC in 2022.

Importantly the Protocol is extinguished by its terms on December 31, 2023. Bottom line: the Protocol is in limbo.

The only way I see to end the divisiveness and have peace is to separate—shake hands, wish one another well, and go our separate ways. [Whoa. How did we get there? I thought we were having an argument. You're thinking about leaving?]

I don't want to stay in the United Methodist Church, given its current trajectory.

The United Methodist Church has left me. [No record of any UMC kicking anybody out, no matter how theologically confused he, she, or they be.]

Schisms are not necessarily bad. [Check that out with the Wesleys and all the Church Fathers in Christendom.]

Christianity arose from Judaism. [A schism?]

Protestants left the Roman Catholic Church.

Methodists split from the Episcopalians. [Which John Wesley fought until his dying day.]

If we disaffiliate from the United Methodist Church, we'll still be Buncombe Street. I see it as a time of unity ["Unity" became a rallying cry for the disaffiliates at Buncombe Street: We must separate from the denomination, vote down and risk casting out all those disagree with us, in order to come together and be unified.] and a time of revival. As I see it, the only way for Buncombe Street to be Buncombe Street is for us to make a new conference relationship. As I see it, if we remain United Methodists, we won't be Buncombe Street anymore.

It is not so much about now, today, and even next week, but the future. Buncombe Street could change quickly as First Baptist has, and Trinity Lutheran has, and Christ Church may. St. Paul's Anglican Church is full of refugees from all three.

Where does our staff stand? [Now things are getting ugly.]

Karen Jones is progressive.

Grover Putnam holds traditional beliefs.

Justin Gilreath holds traditional beliefs.

Brian Gilmer has not stated his position.

Options:

- Remain in the United Methodist Church.

- Join another conference, such as the Global Methodist Church or the Free Methodist Church.

- Become independent.

Frazer Memorial in Montgomery, Alabama, joined Free. Pastor Emeritus John Ed Mathison said we could not go wrong with either Free or Global. [Mathison's Frazer

Memorial would soon snub the GMC and go FMC.] The Global Methodist Church's *Book of Doctrines and Discipline* is essentially the United Methodist current *Book of Discipline* (see hand out). . . .

Significant difference from Buncombe Street's situation is that all of these churches had pastoral leadership and co-operative Bishops.

Fred's summons to revolution, based upon WCA/GMC cherry-picking from isolated, obscure UMC events elsewhere, wasn't prevarication, it was propaganda, akin to that of politicians whipping up fear of immigrants eating our cats and dogs. Fred closed with a prayer citing Isaiah 43:19, telling the Lord to "Open our eyes to see the next step. . . . You've prepared for us. As we have been faithful to the old, open our eyes to the new. Thy will be done. We ask in Jesus's name. Amen."

Then Fred announces his petition:

Yesterday, Monday, April 4, Rev. Brian Gilmer was informed of the committee's goal to disaffiliate or withdraw from the UMC and establish another relationship. He said he would tell the District Superintendent. Rev. Gilmer declined to help the committee as other UNIC [sic] senior pastors have done. The effort to disaffiliate is not an attack on Rev. Gilmer. This process would have been initiated regardless of the minister. It is the committee's prayer that we will find an amicable and peaceable way forward. This petition is a good faith effort toward that end. We hope that you will read this petition in a spirit of prayer and sign it if you share the committee's belief.

After presenting the petition for a Charge Conference to move toward disaffiliation, Fred ended, "We know there are many questions to be answered regarding the future of the church. Buncombe Street has formed a committee (with a web page called 'The Way Forward') to educate our congregation. In addition, the Friends to Preserve Buncombe Street will launch a website very soon to provide reference material and ongoing updates regarding the inevitable split of The United Methodist Church, what other churches are doing, and where we go from here."

Thus began a year in which segments of the congregation debated over whether or not to stay UMC. Rather than have more relevant conversations around pressing questions such as, How can we aging boomers best reach a new generation with the gospel of Jesus Christ? What portion of the mission of Jesus Christ has been assigned to us? What can we do to engage the more than half of our members who fail to participate in our worship and work? Who is there in this town for whom Buncombe Street could be an answer to their prayers? WWJD? Buncombe Street's ascending leaders focused upon its connection to The UMC as if that was the cause of all their problems and a strategy to thrive in the future.

BTW: Separatists like Fred invariably cite Methodism's breakaway from the Church of England as precedent for their disaffiliation, an oversimplification of history. When one considers the mobs and violent treatment of "the people called Methodists," why didn't early Methodists, a lay renewal movement within Anglicanism, separate from the Church of England? Absolutely not, said John Wesley in his treatise, "Reasons Against a Separation from the Church of England." Wesley's first point: separation would contradict what Methodists have been saying about Christ and his unifying power. "We are now sweetly united together in love. We mostly think and speak the same thing. But this would occasion inconceivable strife and contention, between those who left, and those who remained in the Church, as well as between those who left us, and those who remained with us." Separation would encourage "a sharpness of language toward the whole order, utterly unbecoming . . . Christians." Besides, disaffiliation (er, uh, I mean Separation) is an "experiment [that] has been so frequently tried already, and the success [has] never answered the expectation."

Dissension, disagreement is the normal, predictable state for Christians, reminds Wesley. "We cannot be a compact, united body." If there are those among us who are wrong, Wesley says, "We should employ all our care, labour, prudence, joined with fervent prayer, to overcome evil with good, to melt . . . hardness into love." He adds, "We have need of all gentleness and meekness of wisdom. Contempt, sharpness, bitterness can do no good. . . . Harsh methods have been tried again and again. . . . They always occasioned numberless evils; often wholly stopped the course of the gospel."

The church "is the Mother of us all, who have been brought up therein. We ought never to make her blemishes matter of division, but rather of solemn sorrow before God. We ought never to talk ludicrously of them. . . . Rather, we should conceal them, as far as ever we can, without bringing guilt upon our own conscience. And we should use every rational and scriptural means, to bring others to the same temper and behavior. I say, *All*; for if some of us are thus minded, and others of an opposite spirit and behavior, this will breed a real schism among ourselves. It will of course divide us into two parties; each of which will be liable to perpetual jealousies, suspicions, and animosities against the other. Therefore on this account likewise, it is expedient in the highest degree, that we should be tender of the Church to which we belong."

Wesley was as uncomfortable with separation, disaffiliation, and schism as Jesus.

By April 12, the church council received the petition and approved a motion, pursuant to ¶248 of The UMC *Book of Discipline*, to request the district superintendent for a special Church Conference to vote on whether Buncombe Street would like to disaffiliate from The United Methodist Church. The newly created Way Forward Task Force began "a process of discernment" for disaffiliation.

"In an effort to appear objective, they put A. V. Huff and Richard Greer on the Way Forward Task Force as well as long-time member Ida Hudson. They said the experience was awful," recalled one Open Hearts observer.

Disaffiliates were in a rush because there was to be a specially called annual conference in June 2023 where churches voting to disaffiliate under ¶2553 would be allowed to do so. But even at this late date, the bishop and conference trustees dithered about how to allow churches to vote themselves out of The UMC and how much they should pay.

The disaffiliates hurriedly and (at last) publicly organized themselves, utilizing the Way Forward Task Force to legitimize their efforts. Brian Gilmer and Karen Jones remained clear with each other that they were loyal to The UMC. When asked, Justin officially told people that the staff had been told not to talk about the controversy. Yet disaffiliates knew where Justin stood. Months before, when Justin confided to the inner circle that if Buncombe Street didn't disaffiliate, he would leave and start his own independent, nondenominational congregation, the disaffiliates panicked. Mike Smith began weekly lunches with Justin to reassure him that things were moving apace so that Buncombe Street would be at the head of the line to leave The UMC.

"We were in a leadership vacuum," said Mike. Staff in chaos. Low morale. Nobody in charge. "Justin was the only functioning clergyperson in the building." Brian's attempt to quietly lead was dismissed by the disaffiliates as deviousness, a refusal to lead. Through it all, Krista Bannister skillfully led the separatists. Mike praised Krista as "extremely committed," a person of "deep, deep faith. She has been our spiritual lantern in this process for the past five years."

Coleman Shouse and John Redmond hastily convened a small group in opposition to disaffiliation, the loyalist Save Our Legacy group. Their request to use the church email list was refused, so they cobbled together a list, set up a website, and began periodic emails, but not until September and without support from Brian, the bishop, or DS.

That June fuel had been added to the fire lit by The Way Forward with a rumor that South Carolina pastors were already performing same-sex weddings and nobody was stopping them. It was even alleged that

Ben Burt (former minister of BSUMC-Trinity) had presided at one. Karen Jones vainly tried to counter the rumor, saying that there had been no same-sex weddings in the S.C. UMC, especially none performed by Ben. Karen asked the person spreading the rumor to not misrepresent Ben. The member countered, "It came from a trustworthy source."

The ninth commandment be damned. Proverbs 16:28 also comes to mind. Let me quote it for those of you who were raised mildly Methodist like me and may be weak on Scripture: "Destructive people produce conflict; gossips alienate close friends."

In October 2022 Brian Gilmer asked both groups to stop sending information by email. The Save Our Legacy group complied. The Way Forward stopped their emails and instead began mailing "full-color oversized postcards (like a political campaign uses) with beautiful pictures of church families who supported disaffiliation," griped a member of Save Our Legacy.

"Happy are people who are humble, because they will inherit the earth" (Matt 5:5) seemed to be Brian's guiding text; it should have been Matthew 10:16: "I'm sending you as sheep among wolves. Therefore, be wise as snakes."

Maybe Brian's comfort is to be found in Matthew 5:10-12: "Happy are people whose lives are harassed because they are righteous, . . . when people insult you and harass you and speak all kinds of bad and false things about you, all because of me. . . . In the same way, people harassed the prophets who came before you."

The Save Our Legacy group got no help from the denomination it was defending. John Redmond called the S.C. Conference treasurer's office asking for the already published annual conference budget to show the church's historic tie with Methodism. Request denied. "Apparently the bishop did not want us having access to any information that might help our efforts," said John in befuddlement. On vacation that September, John was called by Superintendent Dennis and told that the bishop had directed him to ask John not to seek information of any kind from anybody on the South Carolina Conference office staff.

Organist Vance Jenkins wrote a letter to the bishop, begging him to intervene in a church that was rushing toward division. Vance said his letter was unacknowledged.

Although Bishop Holston had yet to issue procedures for any church voting to leave, the district superintendent, Jim Dennis (my former student, now in retirement), responded to the Buncombe Street petition for a special charge conference by allowing the church to have a "straw vote," a practice unheard of in United Methodism. Jim's clear, repeated directive that the vote would only be a "straw vote" with no official standing, simply a means of discovering the mood of the congregation, was ignored by The Way Forward group from the first.

"I shouldn't have done it," mused Jim, looking back. In fairness to Jim, The Way Forward let him know that if things didn't go their way, legal toughs in Florida were standing by to launch a litigious blitz.

"I was just trying to survive, having never been a DS before. I guess I thought 'this is my job.' I never said 'Bishop, I need you to do more.'"

It feels to me as if the bishop decided, even before the "straw ballot," that Buncombe Street, embedded in politically right-wing Greenville, now under the firm control of powerful, determined, lawyered up, right-wing laity, was a lost cause.

Jim lamented the "lies and disinformation" cranked out by The Way Forward. "They said that we were denying the Trinity, that we couldn't say Apostles' Creed without crossing our fingers, that we were nothing more than a social justice movement who never opened our Bibles."

———

In deep dives into a dozen South Carolina congregations that stayed steadfastly UMC, I found that the major factor uniting them was that each was led by a pastor who publicly defended the denomination and as one put it, "stood up to the bullies" with no help from bishop or district superintendents. Susan Leonard, who years before had begun the "contemporary service" at Buncombe Street (a number of Buncombe Streeters told me they had begged the bishop to have Susan be appointed as senior pastor at Buncombe Street) made an eloquent video defending The UMC to her Charleston congregation. They stayed.

Belin UMC in Murrell's Inlet was besieged by representatives of the WCA, some of whom traveled all the way from Buncombe Street to stir up the congregation and resource the malcontents. Disaffiliates at Buncombe Street saw themselves as having responsibility to disseminate the gospel of division statewide. Without assistance from DS or bishop, pastor Will Malambri courageously championed The UMC. Belin stayed UMC.

I don't understand why Brian, Jim, the bishop, and others who were ordained to defend the faith and good name of the denomination, as well as their own theological integrity, never once found a way to say simply—in a modestly Methodist way, of course—"much of what you are saying is untrue."

Why didn't those in the ministry of oversight say to churches, "You are free to have a no-holds-barred debate, argue vehemently, and listen intensely, but you will never, ever, under any circumstances reduce these complex arguments to a yes-or-no vote that might risk voting some of your fellow Christians out of the fellowship."

But once the ill-considered straw vote was "won," even by a very small margin, the deed was done. A few months later, when the bishop and conference trustees finally got themselves together and devised a plan for disaffiliating churches, they required another, more carefully conducted, official vote, but once the straw vote had been taken, Buncombe Street was out.

Upon hearing of the straw vote, that wasn't to be an official vote, my mind raced back six decades:

When I served as junior high rep to the Official Board of Buncombe Street Church, Billy Graham announced a citywide crusade in Greenville. The whole town mobilized. At the board meeting, grown-ups debated our congregation's participation.

"Bunch of Baptists trying to get a leg up on us," gasped one.

"Graham says that there will be no separation of the races during the meetings." That did it. The board voted to protect our church from Grahamesque miscegenation and refused participation.

After the meeting, as I exited a side door to catch the segregated Greenville bus to go home, down a dark church hallway I heard weeping. I crept down the hall. Light shown from an open door. I peeked in. Our pastor, Dr. Dubose, was sobbing, holding his head in his hands.

Keeping up with the disruptive movements of a righteous God is not for the faint of heart. . . . I thank God that at an early age I got to see what makes preachers cry.

—*Accidental Preacher: A Memoir*, 102

Remembering Church

While I was still too young to know I was a Methodist, my family moved its mem-
bership to the large, downtown Buncombe Street Methodist Church in nearby
Greenville. There, in that vast, neoclassical, downtown cathedral, work begun in me
at McBee Chapel was brought to completion so that I came quite naturally to answer
to the name Methodist, and have ever since. . . . You wonder why I tell you this story
of my ecclesial origins. I do so to admit, right here at the beginning, that my honest
response to why I am a United Methodist is admission that I am a United Methodist
today because ordinary Christian people at Buncombe Street made me one. . . .
I am here because I was put here. . . .

My involuntary placement among the United Methodists doesn't bother me a
bit. We Americans often exalt freedom of choice. We like to think of ourselves as
independently derived, self-made men and women who are who we are because we
decided and chose to be that way. Religion really isn't yours unless you found it
all by yourself, choosing it as individually right for you. . . .

Our glorification of the power of choice overlooks that so many of the really impor-
tant things in our lives . . . have come to us as gifts. We call it "grace." . . . So if I
believe, if I still answer to "Christian" when called, it is mainly because someone
else told me the story, lived the gospel before me in places like McBee Chapel and
Buncombe Street in ways that made me know that this was my story,
my name, my salvation.

—Why I Am a United Methodist

"How would you feel if somebody was poking around your church,
asking questions, writing a book?" Justin Gilreath asked, covering his
anxiety under his Southern schtick. "Got a lot on me right now. Staff

problems. Stuff." He asked if I knew he was sick (Justin had struggled heroically with Lyme disease since he was a teenager), and burdened by other unspecified stress in the congregation. I had heard Justin refer to his sickness in a couple of his sermons.

I told him that the congregation had thrust upon him huge responsibility and that I hoped he was receiving necessary support. "It's like you are being asked to plant a whole new congregation," I said. "From my experience, new church plants are a dangerous, demanding place for a pastor to be. I hope you are getting support."

View of Buncombe Street Methodist Church, Greenville, S. C. — D-7

"Rather than you comin' to the church for an interview" (as I told Justin that Mike Smith had suggested), "I'd like you to visit the farm and just put your feet under my kitchen table." Unfailingly charming, beguiling, and friendly as always.

I had called, August 2024, asking Justin's blessing to have conversations with some of the leaders of the new, "independent" Buncombe Street Methodist Church.

"Believe it or not," I replied, "I think I'm still part of Buncombe Street. It's my church too."

The next week, Justin called a close friend. "Guess what? Will Willimon wants to write a book about my preachin'. How 'bout that?"

———

The church I remembered had been dismembered. Why did I find it painful? I left Buncombe Street decades ago. Or did I? I had been in contact with only a couple of the church's pastors over the intervening years. My mother's funeral, my first year at Duke Chapel, was the only service I remembered well, save the few where I had been a guest preacher. While I'm one of the three bishops hanging in the archive room at Buncombe Street, I've never seen the picture (and probably never will, now that the congregation's archivist has shunned me). A handful of contemporaries remained, though most have been taken either by death or by their determination to stay in a United Methodist church. A Buncombe Street plate, showing the church in rose color, bought by Mother in some long past missions fund raising drive, adorns our home.

While I was sad that the church was no longer part of the denomination to which I had given my life, my grief was more complicated. In the conversations I was having with those who stayed and those who left, in the videos of sermons and congregational meetings, something in me was lamenting for more than The UMC's loss of my home church.

Over the years, in my writing, and my mind's eye, I have shared memories of Buncombe Street:

> Sunday school—where they dressed you in wool trousers to hear stories about Jesus—was somewhat helpful in decoding the world. Mr. Sanders—superintendent of the primary division at Buncombe Street Methodist Church—paid quarters for Scripture memorization. I got my quarter for memorizing John 3:16, "God so loved the world, that he gave his only begotten Son, that whosoever believeth in him should not perish, but have everlasting life."
>
> As an easy believer, I already knew I was a certified "whosoever." But I needed the Bible to tell me God so loved. . . . That the world has been, is being loved is a truth that must be revealed, a truth inaccessible through walks in the woods. . . .
>
> John 3:16 meant that the world in which I roam, the wide woods once fearsome, sometimes delightful, the trees, the pasture, the abandoned

wells and the rocks that surround my house are here for no better telos than love. . . . Mr. Sanders with his pocket full of payoffs for Bible verses committed to heart—evidence of love . . . the whole shebang is for us to love because God loved the world before we, the world, loved God.

—*Accidental Preacher: A Memoir*, 33–34

Mr. Sanders paid us a shiny, silver dollar if we could reel off the books of the Bible, Old Testament and New. I still have that dollar, though I couldn't recite them in order today no matter how much you paid me.

After handing out flags, Mr. Sanders would have us stomp around the Primary classroom singing, "We've a Story to Tell to the Nations," always provoking a rep from the Susanna Wesley Class down below to ascend and complain of the martial racket. "Aren't these children wonderful?" Mr. Sanders would shout over the din. Suck it up, Susanna Wesley. The whooping resumed, *And the darkness shall turn to the dawning and the dawning to noon day bright, and Christ's great kingdom shall come on earth, the kingdom of love and light.*

None of us ever went anywhere, even downtown Greenville, to tell anyone about the kingdom of love and light. Still, God bless you Mr. Sanders for trying to make us missionaries.

I think I remember a big church where I felt secure, affirmed, known by first name, even by people who weren't Willimons. While I remember a host of names and faces, I recall no sermons and but a few snippets from Sunday school lessons. What does that tell you?

Of course I recall Dr. Pierce Embree Cook, senior pastor during my early teens (our preachers, unlike the lowly Baptists across town, were always "Dr."), asking Charles Curtis—during the week, chief of the women's foundations section at Sears—to sing "The Holy City." We loved to watch Mr. Curtis's face turn scarlet, veins bulging, foaming from the mouth as he belted, "*Jerusalem! Jerusalem! Open your gates and sing. Hosanna in the high-hhest,*" shaking the chandeliers, evoking audible sighs among the congregation, "*Hosanna to your king!*" Dr. Cook would predictably be overcome by tears and always only with great difficulty was he able finally to pronounce the Benediction: "Please rise and receive my blessing so that we can get to the S&S before the Baptists, in the name of the Father, Son, and Holy Spirit."

Responding in unison, "Amen," we rushed the doors to beat First Baptist to the cafeteria on Main Street.

Some of the older boys dismissed the spectacle. "Cook only calls on Curtis to sing when he can't figure out how to end a sermon." Still, the opera was wonderful.

I also remember being deeply impressed by the black-and-white movie *Why You Should Not Date a Catholic*, shown on the brand-new, reel-to-reel movie projector bought for the youth. The twenty-minute drama depicted a couple who fell in love in high school, married, and couldn't stop having babies because he was a Catholic and she was not. In response to his perpetually pregnant wife's pleas for mercy the young Catholic husband said, "We've got to follow what the church teaches." They ended in misery.

"What's 'birth control'?" asked Ossie DeLaney on the way to that evening's service.

"We're Methodists! We can use rubbers," instructed either Kenny or Davie, I forgot which. On my first trip to Europe, sophomore year of college, the cheapest way to get there as a student was the dilapidated SS *Groot Beer*. I met a girl from Penn. Leaving the eight hundred other students to their endeavors, we went out on the deck to look at the stars over the Atlantic. Then she uttered those fearsome words: "I'm a Catholic." An ecumenical alliance spoiled by a black-and-white movie at Buncombe Street.

At the end of a one-on-one, contrite conversation with our associate pastor, kindly, congenial Walter McDaniel patted me on the shoulder and said, "Go on home and pray Psalm 25:7." I had to look it up:

> "Don't remember the sins of my youth or my wrongdoing.
>> Remember me only according to your faithful love
>>> for the sake of your goodness, LORD."

———

During her missionary furlough, Eulalia Cook, sister of our senior pastor, regaled the youth, "I hid from the Communists in the trunk of an old Chevrolet that took me to the dock in Havana. No food for three days. Pray, children, for your sisters and brothers in Cuba! The world says we failed, but I tell you, in my years as missionary, I planted seeds that shall one day produce an abundant harvest that Fidel can never kill."

When the S.C. Conference delegates were seated next to the delegation from Cuba, at my first General Conference in Denver, 1996, I asked the Cubans if they knew Eulalia Cook. They smiled, put their hands over their hearts, and looked upward with reverence.

I never forgot Eulalia Cook's witness.

"Hope to hell that God doesn't call me to be a missionary to Cuba," said my buddy, unimpressed. Secretly, part of me wished God would talk to me in the same tone of voice that God used with Eulalia Cook.

At age thirteen, I dared ask our associate minister, Cecil Camlin, if he would be my advisor for the months of requirements leading to scouting's God and Country Award. He agreed to take me on, warning, "We're Methodists, you know, so there'll be lots of reading."

"Great!" said I, precursor of Young Sheldon, but religious.

Meeting every Thursday after school, Cecil plied me with grownup books from the church library. William Warren Sweet's six hundred pages (seemed a thousand) on the history of Methodism. "Methodism is best understood in relation to the history of the American people," Sweet had said. Sweet reported that Franklin Roosevelt called Methodists "the most truly American of all our churches." One Sweet sentence shook me: "The most serious problem faced by American Methodism as a whole was its rapidly increasing wealth."

Then there was Bishop Gerald Kennedy's memoir. Bishop Kennedy didn't brag about his picture on the cover of *Time*. His proudest achievement was braving popular scorn as a conscientious objector in World War II. Somebody's life of John Wesley. Paul Tillich's *The New Being*, though God knows why.

I was told to get a large map and, with red pushpins for the schools, blue for hospitals, to show every Methodist mission across the world. It took two trips to Woolworth's for pins enough to note Methodism's march, covering the globe with more churches, hospitals, orphanages, seminaries, and schools than Sherwin-Williams did with paint. When

I proudly handed in my map board, every corner except Russia covered in pins, Cecil took a quick look and said, "Your source must have been dated. We lost China to the Communists." A setback for Methodist triumphalism. One hundred pins wasted.

Just before Easter I stood before all of Buncombe Street as my mother pinned my God and Country Award badge on my swelling thirteen-year-old chest. "It's kinda nice that my church expects more reading than Hughes Junior High," I confided to my only friend who liked to read.

At that time in my life at Buncombe Street, the Church Year didn't mean Advent and Christmastide, it meant before or after "Church Basketball" at the Greenville Y, practice on Wednesdays with Coach Clontz, Saturday morning games fiercely fought against every church in town, except for the Unitarians. In spite of the occasional exchange of pre-game slurs and post-game scuffles in the parking lot, you could tell we played Christian basketball: they let even a loser like me be on the team. Still, my wound has never completely healed after Ray Clontz—when everybody fouled out against First Baptist—hesitated to put me in the game, figuring that our prospects were better with four players than five, counting me.

At halftime in the game against Saint Mary's, Dr. Cook made a rare appearance in the locker room to rally us: "Boys, that priest is a Polack. If you guys blow this game I won't be able to hold up my head at the Ministerial Association's Pray for America lunch next week. Did you come to win or not? Get out there and stop acting like a bunch of pansies! Beat the hell out of those Papists!"

We didn't.

The year's highlight was the Methodist State Basketball Tournament all the way in Columbia, a spring basketball extravaganza that lasted the whole weekend, breaking only briefly for church at Shandon Methodist on Sunday.

"When is Buncombe Street going to do right and build us a gym like Shandon?" we demanded, after we lost the state tourney, again.

A member of Open Hearts sneered, "At Buncombe Street, getting your kid on one of the church's basketball teams was more important than teaching them the Bible."

Imprinted by my high school memories, I mused, *And your point is what?*

When the pastor could talk the musicians into it, we held a Fall Revival. We all knew that downtown Buncombe Street was too sophisticated to be having "revivals"; our version was just a tip of the hat to our proletarian Methodist roots. One year we snagged Dr. Charles Allen from Atlanta, author of the bestselling, Norman Vincent Peale rip-off, *God's Psychiatry*. Dr. Allen showed up in a blue Thunderbird. After service, the guest revivalist wowed us boys by showing us under the hood and bragging, "I put the pedal to the metal on the way up here, leaving some hick cop in my dust near Gainesville. How 'bout that?"

Everybody I knew went down to the front during the last hymn, last night of the revival, and gave their lives to Christ, or made a deeper Christian commitment, or showed that we were at last serious about discipleship, or to please our parents, or to impress the girls, or something.

As we trooped out, end of service, on the last night of one of these revivals, Freeman Orr, our irreverent, much-beloved, chronically insubordinate organist, called out, "Would you boys get off your butts and get down to the kneeling rail sooner? It's a school night, for God's sakes! I thought Cook would force me to play 'Just As I Am' 'till midnight!"

Because Buncombe Street was big and had money, we had some wonderful, well-trained youth leaders. Ken Argenbright (you can see him there, proudly presenting the youth under his command in the photo of the MYF from Mr. Moseley's *Buncombe Street Story*), though my only remembrance of Ken was his scoffing when a high school student tried to win an argument by quoting the last book of the Bible, "Revelation? Ha! It was one man's dream!" Ken Argenbright, my introduction to historical criticism.

> "How come our church has got all these plaques stuck everywhere? On the windows, the pews, at the bottom of the pulpit, even the piano. Is that because these people paid for the right to have their names on a plaque just because they gave money to the church?"

An elder responded, "We've got these plaques there to remind boys like you that you didn't think up Jesus on your own. Somebody had to tell you, show you. None of this belongs to you by virtue of your birth."

Sweeping his hand over the expanse of the Buncombe Street Sanctuary, he declared, "Boy, you didn't come into the world owning any of this. The names of the dead are stuck everywhere to remind you that what you believe, your salvation, this church—gift. Gift all the way down.

"If this church had done it right, we would've nailed a plaque on your forehead: Here, Courtesy of Somebody Else."

—*Willimon Stories*, 228

The greatest influence upon me was Director of Christian Education during my high school years Olene Civils. Olene was among the last of the Methodist Deaconesses, "Methodist nuns," confided a buddy, "like in *The Sound of Music* but without the robes." We loved Olene's cheerful disposition, even when we youth were not at our best. Although young, we knew enough to know that here was a woman who had given up family, children, just about everything to be stuck with us upstairs in the youth room at MYF every Sunday night after the snack supper at six and the New Year's Eve lock-in with sleeping bags in the fellowship hall. Only a "deaconess" would subject herself to such indignities.

In Olene's tidy, tiny office down the hall, when I confided, sheepishly, hesitantly that I might, just maybe (who knows?), go into the ministry, Olene responded, "Not surprised. You love to be up front, in charge, don't you? Still, if God is calling you, you'll find the study and discipline to be quite a challenge."

Olene, master manipulator of youth on behalf of Jesus.

There was a warm-hearted serenity about the world that embraced me at Buncombe Street, a great place for a kid from a single-parent family. Even though they must have all known that my daddy had left Greenville after doing time in the Federal pen in Atlanta, nobody ever brought it up, a true moral achievement for a church, in any age. Was Olene behind their compassionate silence?

There's no way my Buncombe Street would have voted to leave United Methodism. No group in my Buncombe Street would risk alienating or evicting their fellow church members. Nobody would have called for a vote on what was believed or not. Who would have placed themselves on a pedestal and bragged about how much Bible they knew that the rest of us didn't?

Or maybe "my Buncombe Street" that I bear in heartfelt reminiscence never was.

Nostalgia? *Me?* "Nostalgia" is rooted in the Greek *nóstos* "return, homecoming," a word that figures prominently in *The Odyssey*, which they made us read at Wofford for Intermediate Greek. The Latin word *nostalgia* was invented by a Swiss physician to describe an unwanted medical condition. *Algia* in "nostalgia" means "pain," a disorder first observed among melancholic, malnourished soldiers in which the victim "embellishes the memories attached to places where he was brought up, and creates an ideal world where his imagination revels with an obstinate persistence" (*Appletons' Journal*, May 23, 1874).

While nostalgia is now considered a harmless emotion, an even beneficial pastime for old guys like Stanley, Grant, Rick, and me, who sit around and drink coffee on Fridays, I don't like your accusation of me as nostalgic.

However, if I'm guilty of nostalgia in regard to my home church, maybe my sentimentally warped remembrance that I bear is testimony to the grace I experienced at the church that bore me, redemptive overcoming of sadness or hurt by joy, in the backward glance. And, at my age, if I'm departing the present for the future (i.e., death), then nostalgia may be how I graciously, gratefully let go of past loss and the painful present, making the best of a bad situation by looking back to a time that is as pleasant as I remember.

My favorite 2007 *Mad Men* episode is when Don Draper, 1950s ad man par excellence, hawks the new Carousel Projector. Don proposes selling the device as a nostalgia machine. Starting the slide show with photos of his family, Don tells the gathered ad execs that in Greek "'nostalgia' literally means 'the pain from an old wound.' It's a twinge in your heart, far more powerful than memory alone. This device . . . takes us to a place where we ache to go again. It's not called the Wheel. It's called a Carousel. It lets us travel the way a child travels. Around and around, and back home again . . . to a place where we know we are loved."

While that's too much to claim for a slide projector, maybe my black-and-white, faded snapshots of memories of Buncombe Street are no more than nostalgic. I don't find much of this kind of thing in the Bible, a book notorious, not for its sentimentality, but for its honest remembering and recording of Israel's and the church's past, warts and all.

Trouble is, nostalgia about the church tends to flatten and reduce our images of and options for the church. The church remembered becomes the ideal. The present is simplified, as if our current challenges are duplications of those in the past and are therefore amenable to past solutions. Nostalgia protects us from honestly receiving the present as it is. Worse theologically, nostalgia gives us the illusion that we humans, as well as our creations, shall abide until the end of the ages, if only in our minds.

Maybe my fears for Methodism's future, my sadness at the diminished state of my denomination's present, provoke the slippage of my remembrance into rank nostalgia.

Sure, I'm guilty of viewing Buncombe Street through nostalgic rose-colored glasses. Okay, maybe my treasured best memories blur and bury the worst of it. Still, if memory serves, it helps me to confess who I really am and who my people are, to understand the present without being captivated by it. Could the disaffiliates be as captivated by nostalgia as I? On the other hand, since few of the leaders of the breakup had been longtime members of Buncombe Street, perhaps their illusions arose from elsewhere.

I remember a fun group of youth in the MYF, the in-depth Bible study led by James and Betty Orders, James the son of Mr. J. B.

"I'm all for you knowing more about the Bible," said one of my friend's parents, "as long as you don't take it too far." Too far meant that uncivilized wilderness beyond dignified Buncombe Street, that land that's hostile to all intelligent people, the mean-spirited kingdom settled by the tribe who calls themselves "Baptist."

Ken Argenbright's "The Book of Revelation! It's one man's dream," was the last straw for James and Betty Orders. They had resisted Ken's pressure to use officially approved Methodist literature in the youth group. Now they realized their fundamentalist fight was in vain. Tearfully, they bid farewell to the youth of Buncombe Street and headed toward more conservative Mitchell Road Presbyterian.

James and Betty were the first people I knew to leave a church because of Jesus. All of us youth were impressed that the Orders were paying a high price for their biblical commitments. James and Betty sacrificed Buncombe Street Church, a building they loved and which they sacrificially supported, as well as the youth group that they led so passionately.

Years later disaffiliates at Buncombe Street took another path, untrodden by Methodists. They sacrificed their fellow church members, taking the church out of the denomination to which they, and all of their fellow Methodists, had vowed loyalty. The disaffiliates' affection for church property was a chief motivation for the path they took, even though there's not a shred of biblical support for such love. When you sacrifice others, by making your love of something else more lovable than fellowship with them, that's ugly.

Little did I know that my Buncombe Street was the last gasp of the Protestant hegemony over American life. The world was leaving behind secure, adaptable, complacent, mainline Christianity. Rumblings of disestablishment could be heard by the time I headed to college.

Warned by James and Betty Orders about being tempted to read "a terrible new book, *Honest to God*," by an English bishop, full of unabashed atheism and outrageous doubts, first week at Wofford College I headed to the college bookstore and bought the book.

———

A couple of decades later, when Duke's Stanley Hauerwas and I described the seismic shift that was occurring in American church life in *Resident Aliens*, of course I just had to begin with Buncombe Street, probably the most frequently quoted passage I ever wrote:

> Sometime between 1960 and 1980, an old, inadequately conceived world ended, and a fresh, new world began. . . . This book is about a renewed sense of what it means to be Christian, . . . in a distinctly changed world.

When and how did we change? . . . One is tempted to date the shift sometime on a Sunday evening in 1963. Then, in Greenville, South Carolina, in defiance of the state's time-honored blue laws, the Fox Theater opened on Sunday. Seven of us—regular attenders of the Methodist Youth Fellowship at Buncombe Street Church—made a pact to enter the front door of the church, be seen, then quietly slip out the back door and join John Wayne at the Fox.

That evening has come to represent a watershed in the history of Christendom, South Carolina style. On that night, Greenville, South Carolina—the last pocket of resistance of secularity in the Western world—served notice that it would no longer be a prop for the church. . . .

Our parents never worried about whether we would grow up Christian. The church was the only show in town. On Sundays, the town closed down. One could not even buy a gallon of gas. There was a traffic jam on Sunday mornings at 9:45, when all went to their respective Sunday schools. By overlooking much that was wrong with the world— it was a racially segregated world remember—people saw a world that looked good and right. . . . Church, home, and state formed a national consortium that worked together to instill "Christian values." People grew up Christian simply by being lucky enough to be born in places like Greenville. . . .

A few years ago, the two of us awoke and realized that whether or not our parents were justified in believing this about the world and the Christian faith, *nobody* believed it today.

—*Resident Aliens: Life in the Christian Colony*, 15–16

Shortly after *Resident Aliens* was published, I'm standing on the steps of Duke Chapel, basking in the morning sun, and in my position as Dean of the Chapel. Olene Civils, now a first-year student at Duke Divinity School, preparing to be ordained at long last, walks by the chapel on her way to class.

"Come here," she beckoned, curling her finger the way she used to do at some miscreant back at Buncombe Street. "You boys are not as clever as you think. I know that seven of you cut MYF and snuck out to movies at the Fox. Tell your buddies that if each of you comes to my office and confesses what you've done, I will not tell on you to your parents."

"My parents are dead!" I protested. "And you haven't got an office."

Olene smiled that sweet grin of hers: "I have ways."

How fortunate Olene and I were to have been loved by Buncombe Street, how lucky to have had so many grand opportunities to return some of that love in our ministries and savor it in our memories.

Looking back across my scholarly endeavors, I realize how much I owe to my home church. I received from Buncombe Street not only a gentle, capacious view of the kingdom of God but also a rather relaxed, middling Christian believing. Indulgent. Accommodated. Decorous. Latitudinarian, for good and for ill. My sense that music, especially the great hymns of the church, are at the core of the Christian experience; respect for the doctrinal diversity we had within a mainline congregation; gracious orthodoxy, connectionalist in contrast to the attitudes of the dominant Southern Baptist milieu which, so we were told, was judgmental, condemnatory, belligerent, congregationalist, and separatist. All that, my inheritance from Buncombe Street.

How much of my theology today is attributable to my rebellion against the flaccid divinity I absorbed in my youth? How was *Resident Aliens* my personal disaffiliation from Buncombe Street? My antipathy toward the Council of Bishops, that too?

As a teenager I thought I was making up my mind about God when all the while God was making up my mind through my embrace of, and perhaps more so in my push back against, Buncombe Street that birthed me. My senior thesis at Wofford was "The Anabaptist View of the Church," about as far from Buncombe Street as church history could take me. At Yale Divinity School I wrote a paper for Paul Minear on "Homosexuality in the New Testament," little knowing that I was preparing to tutor those who wrongly felt they knew for sure what the New Testament said on the subject. My dissertation at Emory, "A Study of the Impact of Liturgical Theology on the Local Church," was somehow tied to Sundays at Buncombe Street where beauty, tradition, the hymns of the church mattered more than the preaching.

As he pressed upon me Gibson Winter's *The Suburban Captivity of the Churches*, a fellow Wofford student activist asked, "You sure you want to work for these guys?" I read Winter and thought of an urban church with a suburban soul. After perusing Winter's takedown of smug, white, compromised suburban congregations, I thought, "Who better to shake them up than I, one of them?"

Before heading to Yale Divinity School, I underlined statements from two of my heroes, both of them Catholics: Reluctant saint, Catholic Worker Movement founder Dorothy Day, in *The Long Loneliness* praised those who "live in a state of permanent dissatisfaction with the Church." Greatest American novelist Flannery O'Connor, smirked, "You have to suffer as much from the Church as for it."[1] Of this, I am a witness.

While summering in 1969, as a youth worker at Trinity UMC, Anderson, S.C., I read Jeffrey Haden's *The Gathering Storm in the Churches*. Complacent, established churches (like Buncombe Street?) are in for some rough weather, predicted Haden. With so few things tied down, Buncombe Street may have a lot to lose.

In seminary, the first sociology of religion book I read was Will Herberg's *Protestant-Catholic-Jew* (1955). "It is only too evident that the religiousness of America today is very often a religiousness without religion, a religiousness with almost any kind of content or none; a way of sociability or 'belonging' as a way of reordering life to God."[2] Herberg's characterization of the Protestant congregation as a kind of sanctimonious social club called to mind some aspects of the church that birthed me where it was often hard to tell where ended the USA and began the kingdom of God.

"You better take a look here," advised a comrade rookie my first month as associate pastor at Broad Street UMC, Clinton, SC. I read Dean Kelly's *Why Conservative Churches Are Growing* in one afternoon. Kelly implied that liberal, mainline, thin theology, weak commitment churches (Buncombe Street all over) were doomed when increasing numbers of Americans wanted more out of church than inoffensive, innocuous theology, bourgeoisie respectability masquerading as gospel. Looking back, maybe the disaffiliates had the guts to embrace the change that I feared.

---

1. *The Habit of Being: Letters of Flannery O'Connor* (Farrar, Straus and Giroux, 1979), 122.
2. Will Herberg, *Protestant-Catholic-Jew: An Essay in American Religious Sociology* (University of Chicago Press, 1955), 19.

In my second month as faculty at Duke Divinity, sociologist Bob Wilson (later, my mentor) peppered me with questions about Buncombe Street. Whatever Bob learned from those interviews, he folded into his book (with Ezra Earl Jones) *What's Ahead for Old First Church?* "Glad you had a good experience at Buncombe Street," said Bob, "churches like that are not long for this world."

A decade later, when Bob and I rocked The UMC with *Rekindling the Flame: Strategies for a Revitalized United Methodism* (winning us a full-color front cover of conservative *Good News* and the undying scorn of a dozen bishops), Bob and I named a bunch of congregations, just like my home church, prestigious flagships of The UMC ten years before, that had, by the mid-1980s, closed.

I sent a copy of *Rekindling the Flame* to Jack Meadors, soon to be bishop, then-pastor at Buncombe Street, with a note. "What you're doing, leading a lively congregation, is becoming all-too-rare in the UMC. Large, downtown congregations are a dying breed. Way to go, Buncombe Street."

See why I featured an affectionate reminiscence of Buncombe Street in my *What's Right with the Church* and began *Resident Aliens* with Buncombe Street going head-to-head Sunday night with the Fox Theater, and losing?

Still, neither Buncombe Street, nor anything about it, is eternal. My home church is full of strangers who neither know nor honor me and my contemporaries. We are ghosts. The Buncombe Street that I bear in remembrance is not there, not only because we are mortal and the world moves on but also because a living God, present in the power of the Holy Spirit, refuses to stay still. *Gott nimmer Ruhet*, Karl Barth convinced me. A resurrected God is nothing if not restless.

Here's the way I talked about it in my last book:

> I grew up on red clay, kudzu overrun dirt that my family had worked for two hundred years, baptized into octagonal McBee Chapel Methodist Church, South (no time, in the twenty years since Methodist merger, to change the denomination's name on the sign out front), eventually confirmed into downtown Buncombe Street Methodist Church (which my buddies nicknamed Jesus National Bank because

of its Ionic columned façade). Like many churches, Buncombe Street (so named before H. L. Mencken coined the put-down "bunkum") tried to look two hundred years older than it was, bigger, heavier than needed to con Greenville into thinking that our church had loomed over Buncombe Street since before The Flood.

How comforting to have something that didn't change, hadn't so far as I could tell, for maybe a thousand years. The ancient hymns that nobody sang anymore, except for an hour a week at Buncombe Street, and the ponderous church furniture, bolted to the floor, were predictable, reassuring to a kid for whom most days were unexpected.

"Why do you wear a black robe?" I asked, during Dr. Herbert's inquisition by our confirmation class.

He explained, "It's the way educated men dressed a couple of hundred years ago."

Of course.

I'm sure the sheer there-ness, the irrefutable immutability of the church was consoling to a kid in a Southern town that still clung to the Old South but (so I overheard the anxious grownup talk in the church parking lot) was on the brink of alteration.

My theory is that churches like Buncombe Street try to look stolid because Jesus isn't. (As theologian Karl Barth said, Christians go to church to make our last stand against a living, unsettling God. Sometimes, the building helps with that.) People say they pay us preachers to bring them closer to God but, as you get to know them, the more you suspect they secretly hope you'll protect them should God slide in too close. Those who come singing, "Just as I am," inchoately know that Jesus intends never to leave them just as they are. . . .

My home church left the UMC fearing that it would change if it stayed. They will fail to impose stability on Jesus, or to steady the God who "makes all things new" (Rev 21:5). . . .

Wesleyans used to be big on conversion, Wesley's heart warmed at Aldersgate, our God-wrought sanctification, changing of heart and mind. Now we've got Methodists who "disaffiliate" out of fear that they might be modified by membership in the UMC. Go figure. They forsake a church that birthed them in order to age as they are. Right-wing politics leveraging fear of divine *metanoia*.

—*Changing My Mind: The Neglected Virtue of Faithful Ministry*, 14

So Buncombe Street was changing, jilting my declarations of love, jolting my memories. Odd that I should be discomforted that my home church was transitioning. Looking back, some of my most notable conversions were wrought by God through the ministrations of Buncombe Street, whether or not I asked to be born again, correcting my received theology, even before I asked.

If you head northwest, straight down Buncombe Street, you will eventually hit Asheville, capital of Buncombe County. Keep west and in less than an hour you will be at Methodist Mecca, Lake Junaluska, two hundred acres without an ashtray or a good drink. It was there Christ overcame me:

My Damascus road divine disruption, . . . occurred when I was sixteen. (Christ loves to accost defenseless youth but seems to lose active interest in seniors.) . . . I grew up in an unashamedly, legally white-supremacist culture. Each day I boarded a Greenville bus that bore the sign: South Carolina Law: White patrons sit from the front. Colored patrons sit from the rear. Nobody questioned that sign, especially those who preached to me on Sunday.

[Olene and Buncombe Street] sent me to a youth conference at Lake Junaluska, beloved (alcohol-free, smoke-free, and lust-free) Methodist resort in the mountains of North Carolina.

At registration, a grown-up whispered, "We hear that you are a nice boy."

Obviously the lady had not heard about the intermission of the junior/senior prom.

"Are you willing to room with a Neeeegro?" Ever eager to burnish my positive self-image, I said, "Yes." I was assigned a room with another sixteen-year-old from Greenville. When I walked in, there he sat on the opposite bed, better prepared for me than I was for him. We were strangers, even though his Methodist church was less than a mile from Buncombe Street; he went to a school four blocks from Greenville High and played on ball fields where we never ventured.

I recall nothing of what was said from the podium that weekend, but I'll never forget our conversation that lasted until dawn Saturday night.

Charles told me what it was like to worship at John Wesley rather than Buncombe Street. He described in detail attending a school worlds away from mine, and asked me about life at my school, from which he was legally excluded. To paraphrase Langston Hughes, my Greenville was never Greenville to him.

"Does it bother you that there are laws that separate us, keep you in your place and me in mine?" he asked.

"I guess I never thought about it."

"Don't you see? They want to trap both of us."

By sunrise, I had my world skillfully cracked open, exposed, infinitely expanded, disrupted, ministered to by another who—like Ananias for Saul, . . . —was kind enough to take me where I couldn't have gone without help. I once was blind but now I see. I left Lake Junaluska better than I had been bred to be.

Before heading back to our separate worlds, Charles confessed, "When I saw that the church had forced me to room with a white guy, I was scared shitless."

The risen Christ egging on Charles, even at sixteen, for risky, faithful, color-courageous witness in service to my conversion. . . . Charles summoned to cure the blindness of Christ Enemy Number One, me.

Only the church [named Buncombe Street] would pull a stunt like that, forcing me to room with my enemy who might also be my savior coaching me through disruptive second birth.

—*Accidental Preacher: A Memoir*, 103–4

God bless the church full of sinners that knew what to do with a sinner like me, who received me, conceived in sin, just as I am, but refused to leave me as I was. Praise to the congregation who, though presenting me with a limited, culturally constrained, often disarrayed, in some ways even dead wrong view of Jesus, rendered me vulnerable to the transformative, disruptive, sometimes even painful continuing, converting ministrations of Jesus. Thanks be to the God who doesn't wait for a church to be faithful and adept at disciple-making, and committed to orthodox theology before God condescends to use the bumbling, still-being-sanctified church that God has got. Mr. Sanders, James and Betty Orders,

Olene Civils, all of you, for any of your faults, were commandeered by God to make a Christian out of me. Thanks.

Could it be, even in the sordid muck of contemporary denominational separation, God was busy at Buncombe Street, just as God had been with me?

Dismembering Church

From earliest childhood, I was God curious. Spiritually inclined, I guess you would say. Bible stories, read by my mother each morning at breakfast, were some of the most deliciously violent, perplexing, truthful, occasionally salacious tales anybody dared tell a kid. The bloodier the better. An eight-year-old's day that begins with a boy slingshot conking a giant with a rock, decapitating him and bragging about it to his buddies, is a day off to a good start.

Our big, rambling downtown Methodist church was filled with interesting, strange, and benign grownups many of whom knew my name even if they weren't Willimons. "Sacristy rat" was Martin Luther's name for kids like me with nothing better to do than hang out at church. Working on my God and Country award for Scouts, the preacher slipped me grownup books about Methodists suffering in Cuba or refusing to fight in World War II. There was a day when Methodists were not monotonous?

Ignorant of Paul's warning to Timothy to run away from adolescent cravings (2 Timothy 2:22), I eagerly signed up for church camp. The last night, holding hands and singing Kumbaya as we floated candles on paper plates onto the lake was as close to God and a girl as a thirteen-year-old male could get in those days.

—*Changing My Mind: The Neglected Virtue of Faithful Ministry*

Here's one of the Friends' early broadsides, unsigned, material handed them for free from the WCA.

Be Aware of False Teachings

In the presence of God and of Christ Jesus, who will judge the living and the dead, and in view of his appearing and his kingdom, I give you this charge: 2 Preach the word; be prepared in season and out of season; correct, rebuke and enourage—with great patience and careful instruction.

3 For the time will come when people will not put up with sound doctrine. Instead, to suit their own desires, they will gather around them a great number of teachers to say what their itching ears want to hear.
4 They will turn their ears away from the truth and turn aside to myths.

5 But you, keep your head in all situations, endure hardship, do the work of an evangelist, discharge all the duties of your ministry.

2 Timothy 4:1-5

The Apostle Paul is warning Timothy to be aware of the false teaching of those who don't preach sound doctrine. Paul's warning was prophetic, given what is occurring in the UMC. We are witnessing many in the UMC who are "turning their ears away from the truth" just as Paul said.

Here are some reasons Buncombe Street needs to leave the UMC:

—**The UMC is leaving traditional churches behind** as they transition to a more progressive and less Bible-centric denomination.
—**The UMC is a large, cumbersome and expensive bureaucracy.** The UMC collects more than $54 million per year in apportionments. Some of these funds, including those that go to our 13 seminaries, are being spent to accelerate the transition of the UMC to a more progressive denomination.
—**Buncombe Street spends over $400,000 a year on UMC apportionments.** This money, in many cases, would be better used to support local ministries and missions valued by the members

of Buncombe Street. Many of the spending decisions currently being made by the UMC (on our behalf) should be made by our lay leaders and clergy. Regarding the various UMC charities, leaving the UMC does not prevent Buncombe Street from continuing to fund any of the UMC charities that we currently support.

—**The UMC has interpreted and enforced the Book of Discipline for its own benefit.** This policy is financially and spiritually detrimental to the traditional churches and their members.

—**The UMC is currently making it very difficult** for Buncombe Street and other UMC churches to leave the denomination. Bishops are not consistent in their rulings, and SC is <u>one of only two conferences in the UMC</u> in which the Bishop has not defined an exit path for its churches.

—**At the 2024 General Conference**, the UMC will likely vote to abolish all language in the Book of Discipline that governs the exclusion of practicing LBGTQ clergy and the exclusion of gay marriage. Additionally, changes to the Book of Discipline in 2024 regarding disaffiliation will likely make it very difficult, if not impossible, for churches to leave the denomination at all.

What Can Remain

As the Israelites trusted God in their journey to the promised land, we must also trust God in our journey to disaffiliate so Buncombe Street can continue to be the church we all joined.

To that end, a vote to disaffiliate will allow Buncombe Street to remain:

—A church that believes that **Jesus is the true Son of God**, was crucified on a cross, was dead and buried, and rose from the dead on the third day.

—A church that believes **Jesus is the light, the truth and the only way to eternal life**.

—A church that believes in the words of the **Apostle's Creed.**

—A church that believes that the **Scriptures are the inspired word of God**.

—**A church where ALL are welcomed to join** as we seek God's forgiveness and His grace through our savior, Jesus Christ.

What Will Be

We believe that Buncombe Street will be blessed by leaving the UMC. After separation we invision [sic] that Buncombe Street will be:

—A church whose direction and mission are not determined by the UMC, but are **determined by God** and discerned and executed by the clergy and laity of Buncombe Street.

—A church that is **sheltered from the imposition of a progressive theology** that is counter to the beliefs of the majority of the congregation.

—A church that **remains focused on God** and not on social and political issues.

—A church **significantly less encumbered** by bureaucracy.

—A church that has **control over the appointments** and the tenure of our clergy.

—A church that is **not financially encumbered** by more than $400,000 in annual apportionment costs.

—A church that **enjoys the freedom and flexibility of owning our church's property**.

—A church **more unified in purpose and direction**.

The Call

We believe God has sent us on this journey to free Buncombe Street from the UMC so that we can maintain our proud Methodist heritage and continue to bring others to Christ. God has great plans for us that require affiliating with a Methodist denomination that remains steadfast in its traditional views of the Bible.

We observe that many local, traditional churches including First Presbyterian Church, St. Paul's Anglican Church, Downtown Presbyterian Church, and Grace Church are thriving, and we believe that God is leading us to a place that will enable us to thrive as well.

It is imperative for the future of Buncombe Street that we vote on October 30th to free our church from the UMC.

Most of the congregation ignored the onslaught as determinedly as they disregarded the weekly, official *Buncombe Street News*. Still, a few pushed back against this WCA-scripted rant. In October Jenna Robinson sent lay leaders Stacy Brandon and Chris Foy as well as pastor Brian Gilmer a letter pleading for a "level playing field" in the congregational discussion, complaining about the barrage of postcards some members (not Jenna) were receiving from the Friends.

"This makes me both mad and sad. It's very disappointing that it has come to this," Jenna told them. She ended her email with "PS: Until last week, I would have signed this 'your friend,' but the word *friend* has negative connotations for me these days."

One of the Friends' slick cards featured the beloved, recently retired former staff member David Stubbs. Decades before, Dr. Bryan Crenshaw had gone out on a limb and hired David, fresh out of Clemson, with little training in youth ministry, to be the church's first leisure ministries director. Though he had spent his entire working life at Buncombe Street, David now advertised that the church must detach from the dangerously liberal UMC. Said one of David's longtime friends, "Many felt betrayed that David allowed himself to be the chief marketer for those promoting disaffiliation." When he retired, they named one of the church's gyms for David. In his July 24, 2022, sermon, Justin praised David as "Mr. Buncombe Street."

"Once they got David publicly on their side, disaffiliation was a done deal," said somebody.

Jana Clack, director of children's ministry and then interim director of youth ministry (fall 2022–early spring 2023), was confronted by an angry parent on the colonnade, charging that associate pastor Karen Jones was picking curriculum for the youth that was not "doctrinally sound." Students under Jana's care would secretly film her teaching and report to their parents the number of minutes Jana spent "talking about Jesus."

Chip and Debbie Fogelman were surprised in a meeting of the Revelation Sunday School Class at Janice Holloway's home by the disturbing news that The UMC no longer believed in the virgin birth, divinity of

Christ, resurrection, or scriptural authority, according to the now-forming, more faithful, and purified GMC.

In early October, two weeks before the congregational vote, professional drag artist Queendelighted got a message through her Delightedtobehere website.

> *We would like to invite you to Buncombe Street United Methodist Church.*
> *We are just a few feet away from Café and then some. Please, please come*
> *at 10 AM and ask for me and I would love to introduce you to everyone.*

Signed with the email address of associate pastor Karen Jones.

Nobody took responsibility for the hoax. Karen and Brian were shocked that anybody in their congregation would stoop so low. The Staff-Parish Relations Committee issued a tepid statement decrying the episode, sort of:

> Last week, someone impersonating one of our clergy reached out to a drag queen and invited them to our church during the Sunday school hour. The message requested that the drag queen come and ask for this clergy by name. It seems clear that this action was done in an effort to link the clergy with a particular stance on issues related to disaffiliation. Whether or not one of our church members instigated this activity, let us all agree that deceptive behavior of this kind is unbecoming of who we strive to be. We are Buncombe Street, where we love and support our staff. You don't have to see eye to eye with every staff member on every issue, but where we disagree, please join us in a commitment to do so with love.
>
> To reiterate, the SPRC has no official stance on disaffiliation, other than we want every professing member of our congregation to be present on October 30th.

John 13:34-35 was cited.

Unmoved by the "no official stance" claim, some disaffiliates decried the SPRC statement. Taking sides, they charged. Coddling staff.

So much for a friendly divorce.

Instead of putting their beef with The UMC to a vote, how come disaffiliates didn't obey the Bible and go with Matthew 18:15-17? "If your brother or sister sins against you, go and correct them when you are alone together. If they listen to you, then you've won over your brother or sister. But if they won't listen, take with you one or two others. . . . But if they still won't pay attention, report it to the church."

The straw vote that was not to be a real vote occurred on October 30, 2022, though the church was told this was nonbinding and, at that time, the S.C. bishop had given no pathway for separation. Kids were summoned from college, old folks roused and wheeled in. The church needed 66.7 percent to pursue disaffiliation. When votes were counted, 306 voted to remain in The UMC, 667 to disaffiliate. Romans 8:28 was quoted at the bottom of the official announcement to the congregation, most of whom didn't vote.

Over three hundred members voted to remain UMC but now, by the straw vote, these loyalists were beginning to understand that 667 of their fellow church members would rather have them leave than be independent Methodist with them. Of all The UMC's mishandling of its congregations during this momentous time for the church, the worst was congregational voting. In one church after another, I've heard stories of how voting, regardless of who "won," was disastrous for the congregation, alienating Methodist from Methodist, bifurcating the multifaceted range of opinions within the congregation, reducing complex theological/biblical/ethical issues to you're either with us or you're against us.

Is it bad taste for me to remind you that, in the only instance of congregational voting in the Gospels, we voted for Barabbas rather than Jesus (Luke 23)?

> GREENVILLE—One of South Carolina's largest United Methodist churches has voted to pursue disaffiliation from the denomination when the time comes.
>
> It is thought to be the first and only church in the state to do so. . . . The Rev. Brian Gilmer and the pastoral staff of Buncombe Street UMC, the church noted, "During our recent church conference meeting, we worshipped together, prayed together, listened to one another and shared our perspectives with each other. We also took another step in the ongoing conversation about the future of Buncombe Street United Methodist Church. Regardless of where we stand on what lies ahead for us as a church, we know that God is with us and that he loves us and

calls us to love one another. We also know that our mission to be and to make disciples of Jesus Christ has not changed."

—*South Carolina Methodist Advocate*, November 23, 2022

At the first Church Council meeting of 2023, Krista Bannister reported that the (straw) vote was won by the disaffiliates and now the leadership had a mandate to guide the church out of the denomination. A group called the Disaffiliation Task Force had been formed. Mike Smith, chair, presented a lengthy financial report, estimating that the payment to the conference could be about $3 million and that negotiations had begun with banks for a loan. He accused the conference of knowing that many congregations would leave so it was building up a "war chest" for the future with false claims that church properties were owned by the conference. He reassured the council that Buncombe Street's multimillion-dollar foundations were safely 501(c)(3) and therefore not church property that the conference might try to get its hands on. He stressed the urgency of the situation due to the unrealistic timelines imposed by the bishop.

David Stubbs chimed in that the (straw) vote was "sacred" and that the conference's terms were "abhorrent." Lawyer Bill Shaughnessy shared that the Disaffiliation Task Force had consulted with the National Center for Life and Liberty, a legal organization that serves to "protect and defend Bible-based values." They were recommended by Jim Bannister. Some BSUMC members had by then donated $50,000 to this law firm as a retainer. The National Center for Life and Liberty would offer legal advice to the DTF. Jim Bannister would serve as a pro bono local counsel and S.C. contact with the Florida lawyers. If the bishop was unreasonable and the DTF was forced into court, "we shall win," said Bill.

Lynne Shackelford said that she thought a period of discernment and information sharing was justified. The margin of victory wasn't that large. She also reminded the group that the district superintendent had clearly indicated that the straw vote was unofficial and only for the purpose of gathering information.

Somebody then asked if the Disaffiliation Task Force had considered the "spiritual implications" of separating the congregation. Bill Shaughnessy responded with the threat that if the church became progressive, half the congregation would leave. Karen Jones countered that, in the earlier vote, nobody was voting on the finances or specific arrangements of disaffiliation and that everyone understood it was just an opinion poll. Karen's statement landed with a thud similar to that received by Lynne.

What would happen if attempts to reason with the conference failed? We would go into litigation immediately, said reps from the DTF.

Finally, a word from the clergy: Grover Putnam waxed metaphorical, saying that Buncombe Street was a ship that was tossed by the waves. "We need to move forward." Justin closed the three-hour meeting with prayer.

Grover was a force for disaffiliation, though quietly, behind the scenes. One of Buncombe Street's homebound members, beneficiary of Grover's attentiveness, said that, while "Grover is all peaches and roses," in his visits with her, Grover confided that disaffiliation "was about the power of The UMC over Buncombe Street. Good riddance to those who've left, the church is doing great." She reported that kindly Grover did say that "he hoped people who left had found a church home at Trinity where they are comfortable."

Former Buncombe Streeters now at Open Hearts would say to Grover, "We *were* comfortable at Buncombe Street!"

The Disaffiliation Task Force got busy carrying out what they considered to be the mandate, otherwise known by the DS as the straw vote. The bishop had finally decided (on the eve before Christmas Eve) on a process and a deadline for disaffiliation. Mike Smith was chair. Members were Sandi Wilson, Bill Shaughnessy, David Stubbs, Barbara Tiffin, Krista Bannister, and Tommy Sinclair. Three were lawyers; all were committed disaffiliates. From the first, the task force was at odds with Bishop Holston and his procedures, particularly chagrined by the bishop's directive to have a period of congregational "discernment" and voting. Buncombe Street had already discerned and previously (straw) voted.

The DTF had lawyered up, not because of any legal threat from The UMC but because that's what the WCA told them to do. The lead attorney for the National Center for Life and Liberty was a Fox News legal analyst and Duke Law grad, David Gibbs III, who led lawsuits against

Florida and the Western North Carolina conferences. Both suits were dismissed. David's slogan: "If it's wrong, fight it. If it's right, fight for it." In spite of the text's notorious linkage with progressives, for some reason David's favorite verse is Matthew 25:40. Maybe you have seen David's free DVD on the right to carry a gun in church.

David junior is eager not to be confused with dad, David Gibbs senior, Independent Fundamental Baptist, notorious for his defense of accused clergy spouse abusers and molesters of young girls.

Those on the DTF who bragged about their ability to swallow the Bible whole easily ignored Paul's clear prohibition against lawsuits among believers:

> When someone in your assembly has a legal case against another member, do they dare to take it to court to be judged by people who aren't just, instead of by God's people? . . . So then if you have ordinary lawsuits, do you appoint people as judges who aren't respected by the church? . . . you should be ashamed of yourselves! . . . The fact that you have lawsuits against each other means that you've already lost your case. (1 Cor 6:1, 4, 5, 7)

By February, Mike Smith, chair of the DTF, revealed that he was in negotiations with S.C. Conference chancellor Kay Crowe. She was adamant that the congregation would be required to have an officially sanctioned vote on disaffiliation, with disclosure of full financial costs of disaffiliation before the vote. Chancellor Crowe clarified that the Trinity campus was not a Buncombe Street UMC asset because the deed was never transferred to Buncombe Street. (The disaffiliates claimed the deed was not transferred due to bungling by the conference; the DS contended that Buncombe Street was offered the deed numerous times but declined to receive it.)

Mike Smith said of his experience negotiating with S.C. Conference officials, "In my entire life I never dreamed a religious organization would make us go through what we had to go through for disaffiliation. We had a weak senior minister who had no business being appointed at Buncombe Street. The lay leadership had to take over. It was hard enough to go through discernment, but without a spiritual leader who was active counselor, it was terrible."

While nobody sued anybody, in spite of the $50k retainer, the threat of litigation became a powerful weapon for the disaffiliates against the DS and bishop. In the brief, single conversation I had with Bishop Holston, when I had voiced my concerns for my home church, his only comment was "They threatened to sue me!"

Maybe the bishop's text was Matthew 5:40: "When they wish to haul you to court and take your shirt, let them have your coat too."

When the time came for the second, this-time-official-though-much-resented congregational vote, the specter of expensive, long-term litigation was put forth as a chief argument for disaffiliation: either vote to disaffiliate or condemn our church to years in court.

(Two years after the end of disaffiliation, forty South Carolina UMC congregations, egged on by the GMC, have initiated a fresh round of suits against the conference.)

That same month, Lindsey Wolfe informed BSUMC that she was resigning from her position as director of children's ministries because she "did not wish to work for a separated church with an unknown identity."

Longtime UMC elder and retired Furman professor A. V. Huff got put on the DTF belatedly and begrudgingly in response to charges that the committee was rigged. A. V. remembers task force meetings as "terrible." "Krista Bannister was spouting all this stuff, and I would say 'that's a lie,' 'this is not so.' Richard Greer [retired physician] and I were the only two who resisted the misinformation. Everybody else just sat there. One of the people at my table was chair of the board of trustees. His constant theme was that The UMC no longer believed in the Bible. I kept saying that's not true. He said, 'I have the truth. I have been subscribing to courses in Bible and theology from a preacher in Dallas for last few years.' He saw me as representing the enemy." (The "preacher from Dallas" was removed last year for his sexual abuse of congregants, but that's another story.)

"My sister knows many professors at Asbury Seminary who were thoughtful and caring people (who are now GMC leaders)," said Wofford professor Carol Wilson, Trinity representative on the committee. "Therefore I was stunned by the mean-spiritedness, and the political orientation of the Friends."

Pastor Brian attended, but never spoke.

"Here I am, an old, superannuated preacher and I feel like I'm the only one battling for The UMC," said A. V., sadly.

In March the Staff-Parish Relations Committee informed the congregation that a broken Brian Gilmer was being given a study leave to regain his health. Sandi Wilson, new chair of the Disaffiliation Task Force, told the council that the South Carolina Conference had agreed to extend the deadline for conducting a final vote to enable the Disaffiliation Task Force to handle logistical issues related to severance of Buncombe Street from The UMC.

As for the Trinity campus, the plan was that the BSUMC would be given credit, in the separation payment, for the money spent on Trinity, estimated (though hotly disputed) at between $400,000 and $750,000. Trinity would become its own church once again and remain UMC, while the downtown campus would no longer be a UMC.

See? Why all the lamentation? We're not pushing anyone out of the new Buncombe Street; we're allowing them to take their progressive, unbiblical views across town to our dilapidated satellite, Trinity. A win-win for all.

Lynne Shackelford, alarmed by what she had witnessed as secretary of the church council, asked for a meeting with the district superintendent and conference chancellor Kay Crowe. Lynne presented a list of "concerns": secret meetings to which only certain members of the congregation were invited; breaching of the church's email system; stacking church boards with "Friends to Preserve Buncombe Street"; the drag queen incident; Way Forward Task Force meetings that were neither fair nor balanced, including a hysterical report of a queer Jesus article circulating at Wofford. Even though Brian had asked for a period of quiet discernment, the mailings, which were like those in a political campaign, were besieging the congregation. Then there was Justin Gilreath's praising the Friends from the pulpit on August 7, 2022, for their courage and comparing them to the New Israelites, and on October 30, 2022, saying that he and his family wanted disaffiliation. Lynne worried about the well-being of loyal church members who had been lost. She shared reports that some of the Friends had been spreading havoc to UMC congregations in nearby Anderson. And so forth.

The two UMC officials politely, unresponsively listened to Lynne, then offered her their prayers and the door.

Beginning in late spring, continuing through the summer, BSUMC begrudgingly participated in a "discernment process." The fate of the congregation had already been decided at the vote that was not supposed to be a vote. The newly organized Legacy, stay UMC group was, by comparison with the Friends, small, under-resourced, and denied access to congregational mailing lists.

Said one former conference official, "In South Carolina we never knew who our bishop was working for. There appeared to be complete paralysis." The district superintendents were given instructions "to listen, be neutral, not get involved, and make sure that congregations were getting their paperwork done."

Unlike Bishop Holston, Bishop John Schol of the East Pennsylvania and Greater New Jersey annual conferences appointed a group of trained "Guides," non DSs, clergy and laity who were available to go into any congregation and guide them through a process of step-by-step, informed, fair, truthful discernment. Bishop Schol also made videos and issued a series of episcopal letters in which he calmly, graciously, but firmly said to any congregation considering disaffiliation, "We don't want you to leave us."

Schol's two conferences lost no more than fifty congregations to disaffiliation.

Lynne Shackelford and John Redmond were surprised by an invitation from DS Jim Dennis inviting them to meet with Kay Crowe at his office to discuss the situation. At the meeting the chancellor asked if Lynne and John would be willing to have their names put on some sort of legal instrument that might postpone or slow down the disaffiliation movement. "We, of course, said we were willing to have our names associated in any way that might help," said John. "We never heard a word back from her." Nor did Bishop Holston ever agree to visit or even correspond with the Save Our Legacy group who attempted to keep Buncombe Street UMC.

Lynne Shackelford wrote a farewell letter to her beloved Sunday school class, in which she announced her intention to join those who were leaving Buncombe Street for Trinity UMC. After enumerating the indignities of the past few months, Lynne beseeched her fellow Christians: "Pray for the many people in our congregation who have loved BSUMC deeply, some of whom were baptized, confirmed, and/or married in this church, and others who have worshipped here for decades. Pray that their tears will stop soon and that they can heed Will Willimon's advice that is the title of his recent book, *Don't Look Back*, and instead look forward to more Christian growth in new environments."

"The Way Forward task force was to hold four congregational, informational meetings. Their presentations made me and many, many other people very angry, because they were completely one-sided. It was so maddening to see such slanted presentations. It was all civil, but it just broke my heart to have such slanted, unfair, fearmongering, untruthful things said about our church," said one of those who was being pushed out of the newly forming Buncombe Street.

Particularly galling was Brian's birthday in July 2023. After three hours in the Disaffiliation Task Force, Brian was asked to leave the meeting. "You are no longer welcomed at our meetings," they said. Brian protested that they couldn't have meetings without him, but he left, emailing Jim Dennis about the event. Mike Smith remembers the meeting differently. According to Mike, once Brian was finally honest with the Task Force about his support for The UMC, the group was simply carrying out the will of the church, moving on without him.

John Redmond shot an email to DS Dennis:

Hi Jim,

I know you don't want to hear from me again . . . probably ever!

I have just learned late this afternoon that the leadership at Buncombe Street has informed Brian Gilmer that he is no longer welcome at Church Council meetings . . . effectively usurping his role as "Pastor in Charge" as provided in the Discipline.

I guess I'm wondering just how long the Bishop and Cabinet are going to put up with the devastation of a functioning, successful, effective United Methodist Church that has always been a leading bellwether congregation, in not only the South Carolina Annual Conference, but also across the entire Southeastern Jurisdiction.

Praying for you daily,
John

John's email was unacknowledged.

Brian knew that the separatists were using Trinity to soften the blow of disaffiliation, presenting the adopted campus as a way to make the separation from The UMC appear less painful. Still, Karen and Brian felt blessed to have Trinity as a potential gathering place for people in the upstate who were losing their churches to the separatists. Today Brian sees Open Hearts, new church start successor to Trinity, as "the one bright spot" in all of the sordid mess that was disaffiliation.

When asked, "Is there one thing you would have done differently?" Brian responded, "Looking back, I was going to stay UMC no matter what. Still, I made the decision to lead from the middle. I felt if I lined up with any side I'd push one side away and I think that I tried to lead from the middle. That proved difficult to do.

"I thought I was hardheaded enough to do this," said Brian. He was wrong. The February council was shocked to hear that the bishop had granted Brian Gilmer a leave for "study and reflection" and that Mike Guffey, who had stepped in when Bob Howell unexpectedly left Buncombe Street, would be filling in yet again. Dr. Guffey's role would be to preach and ensure that meetings ran smoothly. Council was assured by the DS that Guffey would say nothing and keep out of congregational disaffiliation discussion. Mike was welcomed; it was now widely suspected that Mike was headed toward the GMC.

Finally, on April 11, 2023, came the last "congregational discernment meeting" in preparation for the reluctant ballot coming up on Sunday. DS Jim Dennis presided, opening the meeting by urging people to be respectful, "make no accusations," and regard all this as a "faith and a heart issue, much more personal than graphs and statistics and such." Ten speakers, five for and five against, would be allowed to share their hearts, three minutes each.

The trustee chair reminded the group that the four hundred people in the congregation had already voted for disaffiliation and that a "Disaffiliation Task Force" as well as the church council had voted unanimously yes.

When church council chair Hunter Reid asked, "Why are we conferencing once again?" he was told that a major new factor was that Trinity and Buncombe Street could now be separated. "This is a brand-new question. The question that will be before us is, 'Should we separate the campuses?'" The prospect that "the investment we made in Trinity campus" would be given credit in the disaffiliation agreement meant that "there will be a church for you if you want to remain UMC." Thus, early in the meeting, it was obvious that leaders were unanimous in support of the separation, particularly now that the Trinity campus was in play to ease the consciences of those who won the vote to separate from the denomination and as a church home for those orphans who had lost the fight to stay UMC.

"What does a no vote mean? Going back to January of this year and being kicked out of the process, forcing us to pursue other means of disaffiliation, that may or may not include litigation."

Financial arrangements? A sum of $1 million, $44,000 to be given as credit for Trinity. An additional $3 million would be owed to the conference. Apportionments, which Buncombe Street stopped paying the fall before, would need to be paid up; they also had a loan for $3 million.

All this business took thirty-eight minutes before entering into the "discernment" portion. Again, DS Jim urged people "to speak from the heart" on the controversial issue of "human sexuality," making opinions about the "controversial issue" the whole point of the discussion. Again, the single issue that was allegedly not the single issue.

The first speaker wanted to know how in the world Trinity, with a Sunday attendance of fifty, annually subsidized with $100,000, would survive.

DS Jim tried to get the group off discussion of financial matters and on to heartfelt questions related to "issues facing our denomination" (even though that wasn't the point of the upcoming vote).

The fourth speaker wanted to know if a no vote (because the previous straw vote was "real close") means that "we don't disaffiliate." He was told that a no throws the church back into unresolved "tension" and possible litigation.

John Redmond came to the microphone and told the DS that he would speak "not from my heart but from my brain and The United Methodist *Book of Discipline*." John, the only person at Buncombe Street, clergy or lay, ever to be a delegate to five General Conferences, read a list of fifteen questions of church law and interpretation of the *Discipline*, addressed to the DS, bishop, and conference trustees, having to do with questions about an equitable separation of Trinity, the dispersion of the endowment, and so forth. DS Jim said he would get answers (but apparently never did).

Bill Parks came to the microphone announcing that he had "been a member here a little over three years" and had "confidence in our leaders" and their efforts to deal with "Methodist infiltration of the left." Bill feared that "the liberals will have a majority." "I believe in the Bible," he concluded.

Jane Peden, presumably countering John Redmond, complained, "All I hear about is money and *Book of Discipline*" when we should care about the Bible. Jane expressed particular fear that people who have left Buncombe Street "[would] be allowed to come back and cast a vote," adding, "we've already voted and decided."

Somebody opined that the vote would be for disaffiliation but even if not, "if there's a legal suit we will win it."

Joan Gaulden spoke for "inclusiveness," saying that's why she came to Buncombe Street. "Obviously this is going through," said a resigned Joan. "I wish you all well. I'll be leaving the Methodist Church. I ask you, who would God turn away?"

Riley Anderson: "Speaking from the heart is what we were called to do tonight." What keeps us here is how Buncombe Street teaches the Bible, "instead of the devil trying to spin the word."

A woman took to the microphone in tears. "I've lost two children. . . . I love Buncombe Street." She told the group, "When you get to the position I'm in I have got to be in a church where Scripture is taken seriously." Fighting back tears she said, "We can't rewrite the Bible." "God created man and woman." "Why would we ever choose to stay in this conflict" when we have the option of Trinity for those who are unhappy with the vote?

Tim Morrisey followed with, "It's not just about a gay and lesbian thing. It's about fitting the Bible into the contemporary world." "This is not about an exclusive church." "What's not going to change is the Bible." "We do love everybody, even though we must disagree. Jesus loved the sinner but hated the sin."

As I watched the meeting on the web, Acts 19:32 came to my mind: "The assembly was in a state of confusion. Some shouted one thing, others shouted something else, and most of the crowd didn't know why they had gathered."

As the one-and-a-half-hour meeting wound down, I was surprised to see Justin pop up, take the microphone and say, "On behalf of staff, the clergy, and this church, I know that everyone is tired. We have a group of leaders who have worked extremely hard to get us to this point." "I'm proud of the Disaffiliation Task Force." Sure, it has been charged that "some things were not done with integrity," but the task force, like all of us "were broken people."

"I'll tell you that if we don't vote yes on this, this church will be torn completely in two. It's already been broken enough. . . . This is an opportunity that I believe the Lord has provided for us, um, to separate as amicably as possible. . . . I will urge you to vote yes. . . . I believe at this point in time if we don't vote yes this church will be in tremendous trouble. If this church is in the middle of litigation we are going to be so sorry that we didn't do this. So I just urge you to vote yes."

After a lame attempt at humor by the DS, the "Benediction Team" was called up. Gentle Grover spoke in an uncharacteristically combative voice: "We have got to vote yes. We have got to move forward. I'm excited about possibilities of this church. I'm excited about the possibilities at Trinity. . . . We have to move on. I echo what Justin said earlier. . . . We have to be faithful to God. . . . And I have to tell you that if we are faithful to him and his word he will bless us but if we are not he will not bless us. I want to tell you real quickly, all of the churches that I have done some research on who have gone through this process and have decided that the Bible is the center of their teaching, they are flourishing and God is blessing them. And he will bless us. But we have to take a stand and say this is what we believe and we are not letting the world tell us how to live. We've got to move on and be what God has called us to do."

Throughout it all, DS Jim said nothing to counter anything or to offer any clarification except that the trustees of Buncombe Street had repeatedly turned down Trinity's deed. "Essentially Trinity is a separate church [and] has always been a separate church, a satellite with its own identity. . . . You have never been legally one church."

"If you vote *no* you are voting to go against the Bible and bless sin" was the assumption that people were left with. No regret for those who would be leaving. No mention of congregational dissatisfaction with any other issue than the issue that is not the issue. Nor did those who wanted to stay UMC mount much of a defense of The UMC or counter any of the "me-love-Bible-and-you-don't" rhetoric.

I wish that Superintendent Dennis, Mike Guffey, Grover, Krista, somebody had asked Buncombe Street, before they voted, *Who in this room are you willing to be church without? How many of your fellow Christians are you ready to sacrifice by your vote?*

All this heart-sharing at the meeting reminded me, but apparently nobody at my home church, of Wesley's words to those who disagreed with him, "If thy heart is with my heart, give me your hand."

If Jesus's heart was in this meeting, it must have been breaking.

At the special service that Sunday, standing the new confirmands in front of the Table, parents, God, and everyone, Justin asked, "Will you be loyal to The United Methodist Church, and uphold it by your prayers, your presence, your gifts, and your service?"

After each confirmand said "I will," the service ended and Justin led the new United Methodists to the congregational vote where they voted to take Buncombe Street UMC out of the UMC.

By a big margin, but with only about a fourth of the members voting, Buncombe Street voted to be UMC no more.

One Trinity congregant groused, after losing Sunday's vote, "Once again this church has shown that the building means more than the love and mission of Jesus Christ. Buncombe Street has preserved its reputation as the best maintained country club in Greenville."

———————

On May 16, 2023 (one day after my seventy-seventh birthday), in the Truluck Room, at 5:42 p.m., the church council met to finalize plans for the transition from Buncombe Street UMC to "independent" Buncombe Street Methodist Church.

Reverend Mike Guffey thanked God for people's willingness to do the hard work of disaffiliation, as if anybody doubted where he stood all along. Hunter Reid, chair, introduced Lindsey Boone who would succeed Lynne Shackelford as the council secretary. Lynne (most conscientious notetaker ever) was leaving for Trinity rather than be part of the new Buncombe Street.

It was reported that congregational reorganization was being guided by the law firm in Florida. "United" would be removed from signage by June 30, though the church could keep the United Methodist hymnals. If someone wanted to transfer to another UMC, they had to let the church know soon.

Hunter Reid, in a moment of candor, reminded the council that though they won the vote, less than a quarter of the congregation showed up to vote; the majority of the membership either didn't know or maybe weren't keen on the disaffiliation that had so preoccupied the council.

Reverend Chris Ashley was quick to say that he had developed a form whereby all members could indicate if they wanted to stay, go to Trinity UMC on Augusta Road, or just be taken off the rolls. He reported that his audit of the membership rolls revealed that of the church's 2,371 members, only 156 had been lost thus far in the process.

The finance committee informed the council that not paying apportionments to The UMC has benefits; finances at the time looked good. Stacy Brandon added that any who want a refund on their prepurchased niches in the columbarium can now apply. Hunter Reid testified that negotiations with the conference chancellor on the church's final payment to leave were almost done.

Council then went into executive session to discuss staff matters. When they emerged, Stacy Brandon moved that Justin Gilreath be appointed as the interim senior pastor once the conference approved disaffiliation. Passed. Bill Mulligan moved that Grover Putnam be appointed as the interim minister of congregational care. Passed.

Krista Bannister, surely in recognition of her hard work on disaffiliation, was elected as the new chair of the council.

Stacy Brandon thanked the Boy Scouts of Troop Nine for the hundreds of chicken dinners they had made for local agencies, first responders, and over two hundred veterans.

Justin took the floor to thank the council for the opportunity to lead the church, though the church needed healing and decisions needed to be made quickly. First decision, for the summer, Justin proposed one traditional service (ending the early service in the chapel) and The Table. The staff was stretched. Using the same pastors at each service helped to build "rapport and community," which would include "consistent communication from the pulpit" and "create synergy."

Then Justin dropped a bombshell: Beginning in the summer, the traditional service would be moved to 8:45, The Table to 11:00. When organist Vance Jenkins expressed concern about how the faithful would be affected by the new schedule, Justin countered with attendance statistics: the chapel, 80 people on average; traditional, 121; The Table, 425. He added ominously that "difficult decisions will lie ahead."

Rob Gage suggested that the church conduct a short survey about worship preferences. Justin warned that now is not the time for stirring up things with a survey. Grover Putnam chimed in that people want decisions now; he supported the Reverend Gilreath's preferences.

Stacy Brandon shared her fear that those who attended the 11:00 a.m. traditional service would feel undervalued, pained by the new arrangement. Judy Mulkey reminded the group that the church had said they would not change the church services. Brand-new interim senior pastor Justin said he did not wish to make an executive decision that could create discord; the council must give him support.

Kristy Ikenberry said the church council should back what a new senior pastor wants. The Reverend Gilreath stated it's essential that he be able to tell the congregation that he had the full support of the council. The strength of the church was "not in the worship time but in members' relationships." Kristy moved to support the Reverend Gilreath's recommendation to have the traditional service at 8:45 and The Table at 11:00, seconded by Rob Gage. The motion passed.

The meeting adjourned at 7:43 p.m. Buncombe Street United Methodist Church was no more.

"They just stole the church and Justin got a lifetime job," said a former council member who vowed never to set foot again in the church he once loved.

In the months afterward, leaders of the new Buncombe Street took pains to convince Greenville that their church was created out of more concerns that the one-issue-that-is-not-the-one-issue. "I understand that it was mostly about the amount of money they were sending off to The UMC," more than one non-Methodist told me.

All I know is that the second "Whereas" in the agreement to separate, the sole reason given in the legal document for Buncombe Street's severance from The UMC, was that the congregation had decided that it "cannot function as a United Methodist Church due to their firmly held beliefs that the denomination has ceased to consistently uphold and abide by its stated doctrine on issues of human sexuality." Surely the law firm in Florida could have come up with more noteworthy biblically defensible rationale than "issues of human sexuality." Or maybe the law firm was simply telling the truth.

"I will say one thing for that law firm in Florida; they know how to cut a deal," said an attorney to me. "The real estate was worth at least 50 million. The disaffiliating church got the deed for three."

"The smartest thing the Friends did was to hire those renegade lawyers from Florida," said a now ex-Methodist retired Greenville lawyer.

"They set the tone from the beginning. Give us what we want, or we will sue. I'd give anything to know if the conference attorney was told what to do by the bishop or if it was the legal threats. One of the biggest give-aways was the 14 million in endowments. What a deal she gave them!"

The next month, the 2023 S.C. Annual Conference approved Buncombe Street's departure from the denomination, "due to their firmly held beliefs . . . on issues of human sexuality," going through the charade of closing BSUMC as if it had died—wink, wink—and handing the deed to the conference trustees who then handed the deed right back to the new Buncombe Street trustees.

Digression: The Alabama-West Florida Annual Conference, fearing that Bishop Holston would use ¶2549—declaring a church dead rather than disaffiliated—in their conference, as he did previously in South Carolina, asked the Judicial Council for a declaratory decision on the practice.

In October 2024 the council issued Decision No. 1512:

> Connectionalism is a bedrock principle of United Methodist constitutional polity, and the Trust Clause is its foundational element. Disaffiliation is a radical departure from connectionalism. . . . ¶2549 cannot be construed or used as legislation permitting the "gracious exit" of local churches because it applies to church closure and the sale of property, not disaffiliation. Any application of ¶2549 to that end would be a misapplication of Church law. . . . The use of ¶2549 in this way is another failed attempt to circumvent the trust clause, a hallmark of United Methodist polity.

Few were surprised that Bishop Holston's disingenuous use of ¶2549 was ruled unconstitutional, an unlawful "attempt to circumvent the trust clause," but it was seventeen months too late to save Buncombe Street for The UMC.

The Trinity campus was released from its adoption by BSUMC and a new church start began down on Augusta Road. The bishop appointed Karen Jones as the first pastor, Jim Patterson Sr. as administrative pastor. Karen called upon ten laity to serve as a leadership team, some from the prior Trinity congregation, others were Buncombe Street refugees.

When thirty-five laity showed up for a workday to prepare the building for its new beginning, they discovered that staff from Buncombe Street had stripped Trinity of basic supplies, furnishings, and the entire church library.

Nobody ever said divorce was easy.

In the disaffiliates' Scripture slinging, never was quoted: "I give you a new commandment: Love each other. Just as I have loved you, so you also must love each other. This is how everyone will know that you are my disciples, when you love each other" (John 13:34-35). I hear the disaffiliates respond, "When we said we were for 'biblical authority,' we didn't mean John 13."

I'll never understand why the stay UMC, Legacy group didn't engage the wrongheaded biblical interpretation of the disaffiliates. Some of the progressives I interviewed didn't mind calling their foes racist, homophobic, and exclusivist, but few called them ignorant interpreters of the Bible, which could be easily shown. It was as if the progressives were willing to cede "biblical authority" to them. (To be fair, retired UMC elder James Ellis Griffith made repeated attempts to argue biblical interpretation with the disaffiliates but was rebuffed. When Brian denied him the opportunity to give talks on "What the Bible Really Says about Homosexuality," James Ellis had to be content with offering a series to friends in the choir.) The disaffiliates succeeded in ignoring the reality of different, legitimate interpretations of the Bible and in casting the argument as "Bible or no Bible."

What happened at Buncombe Street was no spontaneous outpouring of the Holy Spirit; it was a carefully, expertly orchestrated campaign. Disaffiliates at Buncombe Street, coached by the WCA and the GMC, were Johnny-come-latelies to the work of removing people and assets from an established denomination. Back in 2000, the Institute of Religion and Democracy, a right-wing, Christian nationalist–leaning online organization, announced its multimillion-dollar plan to dismantle The United Methodist Church, along with the Episcopal and Presbyterian churches. The UM Action wing of the IRD said its purpose was "reporting, analysis, and exposure of national church activities. . . . Organizing and training of church activists; and coordinating the efforts of conservatives." Gay marriage would be the wedge issue.

The IRD's efforts are recounted by Sheldon Culver and John Dorhauer in their 2007 book *Steeplejacking*. Few at Buncombe Street had a clue that they were the latest chapter in a two-decades-long national campaign of the IRD (and its younger comrade, the WCA).

The playbook for the takeover at Buncombe Street had been perfected by the tactics of the IRD and WCA with people trained, funded, and encouraged to steeplejack churches in order to overthrow "liberal leadership." As one loyal Buncombe Streeter put it, "We were unprepared for their ferocity. We came for a game of touch football; they played NFL tackle."

Or as one Texas bishop described the takeover of her conference by the WCA, "I brought a knife to a gunfight."

Buncombe Street had a niceness problem. Controversy was rare in its life together. When the battle began, the defenders of The UMC were unable to distinguish loving critics of the church from those who sought to divide and destroy. The progressives (inappropriate designation for the mild-mannered, UMC defenders who worked to keep Buncombe Street's denominational identity as it was) were slow to take seriously the Friends' upfront manifesto: we've had it with arguments; we're leaving and taking this church with us. If you don't like it, see you in court.

The traditionalists (inappropriate term for those who were overthrowing two centuries of Methodism) realized that there was no way to get a church out of connectionist Methodism without creating a truly congregationalist church that's unaccountable to a bishop or any other congregation. The centerpiece of congregationalism? Congregational voting.

Steeplejacking identifies the pattern for a secessionist takeover: (1) Long-term internal conflict in the congregation. [The one divergence of Buncombe Street from the *Steeplejacking* model. Maybe internal conflict had been repressed?] (2) Pastoral leadership is in transition or weak. [Buncombe Street all over.] (3) A handful of church council members make decisions. [Check.] (4) The congregation is isolated from other churches and associations. [Connectionalism trashed.] (5) The congregation is generally unaware of the emerging sentiment to separate from the denomination. [Secret meetings and emails. Sound familiar?]

Once the secessionists (an inflammatory term in South Carolina, still, I think it fits) gather a dedicated, like-minded group of activists, sides are taken, and the core group recruits allies. Those who are not with us are against us. Multiple worship services give leverage for the small group to take over leadership of one of the services in order to form a congregation within the congregation. The disaffiliates demand that the church create a committee to "explore," "share information," and "listen to the congregation." The committee then provides the church with "information" that's always generated by organizations outside the congregation or denomination. The information is always biased, distorted, and replete with wild examples claiming that these cherry-picked outrages represent widespread beliefs and practices throughout the denomination.

The materials invariably list what the separating group claims to be the few chief historic, absolute, orthodox, evangelical beliefs of the church. Then these allegedly core beliefs are contrasted with the heretical ideas that are claimed to be emerging all over the denomination. "Did you know that your denomination is now in the hands of those who don't believe what the denomination has always claimed it believes?" "Here's what's happening in the seminaries that we pay for." "Our denomination is run by people who want to change our historic doctrines!" The objective is to create unrest and disease in the local church and to characterize the fight as a debate to preserve biblical authority. As you can see, the Friends group made no contribution to the steeplejacking playbook.

In every case, say Culver and Dorhauer, the pastor eventually resigns, retires, or is fired.

The disaffiliates at Buncombe Street hitched on to this predictable, trans-denominational strategy for separation. Their rapid success in rallying a stable, content congregation to separate indicates either the weakness of United Methodist loyalty, the power of the surrounding political climate, the devastation of COVID, indecisive pastoral leadership, the tepid response of denominational hierarchy, or maybe a combination of all.

Steeplejacking speaks of "the pastor as pacifier" type. The pastor, fearful of taking a side, trying to be a non-anxious presence, floating above it all; the posture of the well-meaning senior pastor at Buncombe Street who got run over because he was in the middle of the road.

What might have been done at Buncombe Street that could have led to a different outcome?

Culver and Dorhauer's alternative to "pastor as pacifier" is "pastor as protector." When a pastor courageously steps up and tries to protect the congregation from nefarious external influences, often the pastor is surprised by how many allies there are. Because congregations tend to value stability and protection of the status quo, pastors who protect homeostasis are often at an advantage. Duly appointed pastors have more denominational knowledge and loyalty than anybody else in the congregation, and have been educated, prepared by, and vetted by the denomination, so if there is anybody who should speak a good word for the denomination, it will be the pastor, unless the pastoral staff is like Buncombe Street's, mostly a group of clergy who have sidestepped denominational vetting.

Steeplejacking advises those who would preserve their congregation for the denomination: Take the attack seriously. Name inappropriate behavior and ask would-be separatists to stop or to leave the congregation. Identify allies. Stand up to bullies. Niceness is too often the way a congregation accommodates itself to abusive behavior in the church.

Calls to cut funding to the denomination are red flags. *Secrecy is the greatest ally of separatists and their chief modus operandi.* Secret meetings or surreptitious communication must be called out. Don't let agitators hide their identity or refuse to sign inflammatory statements. Say the names of those who are causing the unrest and confront them. *Remember that their behavior is not primarily about theology or Scripture; its chief intent is to take control of the property and assets of the church.* Pay close attention to material that is being distributed and call out lies and distortions.

Above all, Culver and Dorhauer say that churches must *resist calls to take a congregational vote.* Voting terminates the conversation, forces the choosing of sides, and tends to divide rather than foster consensus. Keep talking, arguing, sharing, listening, and seeking until some sort of consensus is reached about how to handle the conflict and those who are producing it. But do not put things to a vote.

Steeplejacking says that once a congregation forms an "independent, fair, research committee," things have gotten dangerous. The questions raised in this committee, and the answers given are designed for disruption. "Do you think gay marriage is biblical?" Then someone, somewhere in the denomination is quoted, then it is argued that soon this will be forced down the congregation's throats. Never does the "research committee" raise vitally important, truly relevant missional questions like, "What portion of the mission of Jesus Christ has been assigned to us and how do we accomplish it?" or "How can we hitch on to what Jesus Christ is already doing in this neighborhood to reconcile the world to himself?"

Successful steeplejacking requires either disgruntled, fiercely crusading laity, or the leadership of "an aggressive pastor" who is at odds with the denomination. I began my study of Buncombe Street thinking that this disaffiliating congregation was exceptional. In most cases in South Carolina, disaffiliation was pushed by resentful pastors who were embittered because they felt insufficiently affirmed by the denomination that had ordained them, Saint John's Methodist in Aiken, South Carolina, being a prime example. This wasn't Buncombe Street.

Then I noted that *Steeplejacking* warns that a fateful step is to "hire a pastor who is not authorized by the denomination." We now know that Justin was being too humble in characterizing his role as a mere loving observer of the process; the same goes for Grover and Janice.

At the close of Mike Guffey's interim, last Sunday (in which Mike joshed, "I've been here three months and haven't been asked to preach at The Table because Justin is stingy."), Mike asked Grover and Justin to come forward. "I can't think of two better people to serve this church at this time," installing them as if he were a bishop and they were United Methodists, as if nothing had happened.

———

Mid-September 2024, someone in leadership of the new Buncombe Street ordered everyone to stop returning my phone calls (following the WCA playbook even in victory), though I was never told why. One leader apologetically explained that they were concerned about the "non-deprecation clause" they had signed with the conference in the final separation agreement. The conference attorney had no knowledge of such a restraint, laughing at the very idea.

"I don't understand all of this paranoia about secrecy," said another congregant. "What have we to hide?" And yet, secrecy, subterfuge seems to be at the core of the WCA, GMC playbook.

I made one last attempt at conversation with the disaffiliates who were now in charge at Buncombe Street. When a lay leader demanded, "Just what are the questions you want to ask?" I responded:

> Here are some of my questions after conversations with lots of folks at BSMC and Open Hearts:
>
> 1. The secret meetings. When did they begin and why was there a need for secrecy and selective communication within the congregation?
>
> 2. Is it true that members of the Friends group attended a couple of WCA national events? What role did the WCA play in the work of the Friends?
>
> 3. Was pastor Brian Gilmer asked to leave a meeting of the Disaffiliation Task Force?
>
> 4. Some members of Open Hearts dispute the amount that was credited to Buncombe Street for money spent on Trinity. They also report that, when the disaffiliation happened, staff from BSMC came and took the library and other materials from the Trinity building.
>
> 5. How soon in the process did the disaffiliating Friends begin having regular contact with Justin Gilreath, knowing that he was in favor of disaffiliation? When did Justin tell the Friends that he would leave Buncombe Street if it didn't disaffiliate?
>
> 6. How would you characterize your dealings with the conference, bishop, and chancellor?

7. Did anyone counter the claims of the Suggs memo asking for a petition for a church conference, or the other charges brought against The UMC by the Friends?

8. What's the estimated number of those who left Buncombe Street after the vote?

9. I have heard from many who left that "no one at Buncombe Street expressed regret that we left or tried to get us to stay." Is that true?

10. I've heard Justin Gilreath preach biblical interpretation and doctrines that are counter to anything I've heard preached in Methodism. Is there acceptance in the congregation of beliefs like the rapture, the substitutionary atonement, the dangers of Halloween, the reality of hell for those who have not personally, publicly accepted Jesus Christ as Lord and Savior, and so forth?

11. I think I detect some shifts in Justin's theology, judging from some of his earlier sermons and his Erskine dissertation. I also note that he said he did not enjoy his time at Duke Divinity. I'm eager to ask Justin about the major influences on his theology, his conversion at the Promise Keepers rally, his indebtedness to Baptist theology, and so forth.

12. Are there any beliefs that are asserted in the UM *Book of Discipline* that are contrary to the beliefs of the present leaders at Buncombe Street?

13. Do you expect Buncombe Street to join a denomination?

14. I've heard that Buncombe Streeters have had much contact with other UMCs urging disaffiliation (Trinity, Anderson; Belin, Murrells Inlet; etc.). How much did leaders from Buncombe Street help other churches disaffiliate?

15. How do the present leaders describe the mission and purpose of the new Buncombe Street? I've read the mission statement, read through the council minutes, and seen all the church's public communications, but I can't detect a connection between Justin's preaching and the character and direction of the congregation.

16. Are there things that you wish you had done differently in the process of disaffiliation? Any regrets? Anything that the congregation will miss in its severance of ties with The UMC?

I've got other questions, but these are some of the key ones that have arisen thus far in my look at events at Buncombe Street over the past couple of years. While personal contact is preferred, I'll also understand if folks would like to respond to these questions in writing. I know your time is valuable; you've got a new Buncombe Street to form.

I will say again that I think the story of Buncombe Street is remarkable in that at my home church, unlike any other church I've studied in S.C. Methodism, laity took the lead, a testimonial not only to unfortunate episcopal oversight but also to the tradition of strong lay leadership at Buncombe Street.

Will

Even though my picture was on their wall, my dear mother's funeral was there, and I once enjoyed the benefits of being a favorite son, I never got a reply.

"Been Tryin' Ten Years to Get You to Say 'Amen'"

My image of the church was instilled in me by the two-thousand-member church I grew up in during the 1950s—a stable, secure-looking fortress that was designed to look more like a bank than a House of God, appearing eternal, fixed, socially and culturally significant, the kind of building God would build if God had the money. If this church had a problem, it was that it was a great sleeping giant. My task was to kick this vast sleeping giant in the seat of the pants, to make America a better place in which to live.

And yet, when I encountered my first churches in rural Georgia and South Carolina, they were anything but sleeping giants. Here were people hanging on by their fingernails, barely able to survive. And their survival needs were not merely financial but also theological. We didn't know why we were there. . . .

That great, fortress-like First National Bank of God where I grew up as a child was now on the ropes. In the space of about two decades that once seemingly secure Protestant Christian hegemony over American life was ending. . . . The mainline had become sidelined.

> —"Up from Liberalism," in Martin B. Copenhaver, Anthony B. Robinson, and William H. Willimon, *Good News in Exile: Three Pastors Offer a Hopeful Vision for the Church*

Of all the anomalies in the way the United Methodist clergy appointment system is administered, the strangest is that most Methodist preachers are appointed by bishops and district superintendents who have never heard an appointee preach. Even though congregations routinely say that preaching is the skill they most crave in a pastor, even though sermons are a major means of pastoral leadership, though Jesus came preaching (Matt 4:23), and though the sermon is the main event of Sunday worship among Methodists, most clergy are appointed by bishops with no knowledge of, or much interest in, their preaching.

One of the few good intentions I followed through with was my promise (to my model, Bishop Ken Carder) that I would never appoint a full-time pastor to any church of over a hundred members, without having heard that pastor preach.

Every January the district superintendents sent me tapes and CDs of two sermons from pastors who might be up for a move that spring. I listened to those sermons, then sent each pastor my response to what I heard. Whether they wanted it or not. The practice led to some of my most fruitful conversations with pastors.

I could find no former district superintendent who had heard a sermon by the pastors assigned to Buncombe Street. Their lack of knowledge of what was being preached at one of South Carolina's most prominent United Methodist churches is all the more remarkable since the distinctive preaching that was being heard at The Table is said by many to be a major factor in understanding what happened at Buncombe Street.

All sides agree that there's no way to assess Buncombe Street's disaffiliation without reckoning with the warm, engaging personality of preacher Justin Gilreath. In just a few years, Justin's preaching dramatically transformed a rather conventional, staid, United Methodist church, spectacularly expanding participation in contemporary worship at The Table, and subtly but powerfully empowering, encouraging, and equipping a small but fiercely determined group of lay leaders, setting the stage for schism from Methodism. Justin's death was a tragedy for his young family, a saddening shock to us all, a devastating blow to the people of Buncombe Street, a loss for the church of Christ, and an instance of the failure of the Methodist system of clergy vetting, care, support, and oversight.

In my one, brief telephone conversation with Justin in the summer of 2024, Justin modestly said he was just a country boy who was as surprised as anybody by his success at Buncombe Street, considering his age and background. "I'm feeling kinda overwhelmed by all that's being laid on me. And the staff! Not a good time to talk." Disaffiliation? "I give all the credit to the hard work of an amazing group of laypeople. I just preached the Bible."

Looking back on that dialogue, I'm haunted by Justin's comment, "I'm feeling kinda overwhelmed." I wish I had found a way to follow up with some supportive comments. Why didn't I pick up on Justin's plea when he said, in so many words, that, now that he was senior pastor, the church and its staff were putting more on his back than he could bear? Justin had clearly entered turbulent waters where he was over his head but could not find a way to swim out.

From conversations with the laity, and the 120 sermons I viewed on the web, I agree that Justin was a remarkable preacher. Every sermon well planned, enthusiastically delivered, in no more than twenty minutes. Yet even granting his homiletical skills, I still don't fully understand why so many, particularly at a church like Buncombe Street, appreciated his preaching. Maybe the positive receptions of his sermons is due to the Holy Spirit.

The same month that I delivered "Being Saved at Buncombe Street," Justin preached that because he grew up in the Methodist Church, nobody told him that, even if baptized, he "wasn't saved."

"A bunch of Baptist men" invited sixteen-year-old Justin to a Promise Keepers rally in Atlanta. "It was the first time in my life that I had ever heard the gospel preached to me," the gospel being that "I had heard that I must repent of my sins and be saved."

In a stadium of six thousand Promise Keepers, with heart pounding, Justin came forward. "Because I was a Methodist," he hadn't a clue about what he was supposed to do. The man down front told him that he must verbally confess Jesus Christ as his personal savior. Justin replied that Methodists baptized him as a baby. "That doesn't count," said the man. Returning from Promise Keepers, Justin asked the pastor of his rural

Methodist church to baptize him again. He was told, "We're Methodist. We don't do that."

In a moment Baptist and Methodist views of baptism "came together" for Justin. As he explains it in this sermon, "In The United Methodist Church the emphasis is put on God choosing you, prevenient grace," whereas the Baptist Church emphasizes "your choosing God."

"Just because you were baptized as a baby [90 percent of the folks at The Table, I'd guess] it doesn't mean that your salvation is secure." You must make a decision for Jesus. While "it is not about the water," he complains that he's tried to talk Buncombe Street into baptismal immersion—his cattle trough is at the ready—though he hasn't had much luck.

"Y'all know that this denomination has got a lot of problems right now, but that's another sermon." As was his unvarying practice, Justin avoided mention of specific denominational "problems" and, as always, concluded with a call for confession of sin and repentance.

The sort of sermon that the Buncombe Street in my day told me we had risen above.

———

I wish I could have learned more about the changes that occurred in Justin's presentation of the gospel. In his writing and the couple of sermons I could find from his early days, I don't hear the somber, substitutionary atonement themes that dominate his preaching during the disaffiliation years at Buncombe Street.

A ministerial intern from Justin's early years told me, "Back then, Justin preached feel-good, nonbiblical, simplistic sermons, about how to be happy in your job, family, and relationships. Little Bible in 'em." Unfortunately, those sermons are not on the web. "His final sermon that I downloaded," said one Methodist preacher, "was nothing like the Justin I knew in our student days at Duke. I was flabbergasted." Did Justin's preaching become more intensely biblical (as he construes "biblical") under the coaxing of behind-the-scenes disaffiliates? Or did the affirmation of the conservative disaffiliates encourage Justin to at last be the preacher he felt all along called to be?

When that same intern preached on the assigned Gospel lection, John 8:1-11, stressing Jesus's mercy for all sinners, asking his listeners to reflect on the ways we marginalize people in ways that Jesus doesn't, a number of people told him how impressed they were by his sermon, one saying, "It's wonderful to hear a preacher speak about contemporary application of the gospel."

Monday morning the intern received an email from Justin saying that he had complaints about the sermon and that, in the future, the intern should "stay away from politics."

Justin frequently describes sin as "brokenness" and we're all "broken people," but rarely are specific sins named, a pale imitation of orthodox "original sin." Never are radical changes in lifestyle recommended; Wesleyan "sanctification." Occasionally he tells The Table that they need to be faithful in marriage, be less materialistic, to dress appropriately at the gym, read their Bibles, attend church, watch their language, and be careful who they date. But in most sermons, mundane morality takes a back seat to urgent evangelistic soteriology because, as Justin says, "Good won't get you to heaven."

———

Justin always conveys an intense appreciation of and love for Scripture, along with a conviction that Scripture is definite, clear, uncontested in its meaning, and immediately applicable to a few aspects of our personal lives, though requiring perceptive interpretation by an informed student of the word before it can speak to less knowledgeable biblical readers like us.

In his January 21, 2024, sermon, Justin boasts to the now-disaffiliated Buncombe Street, "If it's in the Bible we will do it; if it's not in the Bible we won't do it. . . . [Divorce, accumulation of material possessions, self-defense, charging interest on loans?] We stand on the Bible. We stand on God's word."

But Justin's Bible is the meager result of what's left after passing all biblical texts through a rigid, limited theological filter. Little material from the Gospels captures his interest. Matthew 5, the Sermon on the Mount, is never mentioned even though it was the centerpiece of Wesley's canon.

1 Corinthians 13? Romans 8? Jesus's parables? The Psalms? Passages that are uncongenial with Justin's theological preconceptions are ignored.

Almost every text is read as a call publicly to confess your individual sin ("brokenness") and establish an individual, personal relationship with Christ in order that your death can be cured by going to heaven.

On Christmas Eve 2023, Justin preached that while he was excited about Christmas, more thrilling was that "Jesus Christ died. We gather to celebrate the story" that we "have a chance to have life everlasting." As he invited people forward for Holy Communion, he reiterated that "the only reason we have to come to this table is Jesus Christ died for us." (On Christmas?)

Easter 2024, Justin opened with startling threats of hell, gnashing of teeth, and heat, saying that someone told him "you need to talk about hell even more." "I will." (On Easter?) Jesus came to be killed in sacrificial atonement for our sin, the only path to eternal life. "If that's offensive, sorry, that's the truth." Don't delay. Death is a fact. Make a decision for Christ today in order to assure your eternal salvation, if you haven't decided yet. (Judging from the meager responses to Justin's Sunday altar calls, I gather that most of the crowd at The Table had either previously decided or didn't want to show it in public.)

February 18, 2024. "We don't talk much about the blood of Christ in the Methodist Church. You've got to go to a Baptist church to hear about the blood." Because of our sin, God has condemned us to death; Jesus is the sacrificial lamb whose blood atones for our sin, "just like a substitute teacher substituted when your teacher was away."

Jesus's life and death are reduced to animal sacrifice in which the personality of Jesus, his morality, his outrageously gracious welcome and forgiveness of sinners, his relationships with his disciples and the crowds, his teaching and sermons, his resurrection and presence are overlooked. No sweeping Pauline affirmations of the universal triumph of the crucified Lord. Jesus is born, trudges silently to his death, and dies on the cross, and thereby enables individuals who are wise enough to believe in the benefits of his death to get our ticket to heaven.

No John Wesley, either. Wesley was impressed by Jesus's answer to his critics' question: "How come you're always partying and welcoming sinners?" (Luke 15). In response, Jesus told stories about the seeking shepherd who searched until he found the one lost sheep, the woman who turned her house upside down until she found her one lost coin, the father waiting to throw the biggest party this town's ever seen—for a wastrel of a son. Salvation not based on what we do or decide but on God's active, present, sacrificing, seeking, and searching for us, the good news that transformed early Methodists into seeking, searching evangelists.

Suddenly I remember Dr. Cook's sermon (preached between 1958–1960), "The Most Wonderful Word in the Bible." The word? *Until.* The shepherd searched until . . . , the woman sought until . . . , the father waited until. . . . Thanks, Dr. Cook, for celebrating Wesleyan soteriology: God's loving desire to have "all people to be saved and to come to a knowledge of the truth" (1 Tim 2:4). That's the story we have to tell to the nations. Thanks, Mr. Sanders.

In the last of his series on Leviticus, October 27, 2024, Justin summed up Leviticus as "these people are gettin' a whuppin'." Still, because we're Methodists, "We believe we have free will to decide the outcome of our lives based on our decisions." Though "God knows your fate, he gives you free will." Sure, God would like to save you from eternal damnation when you die but as God's children, "If you don't brush your teeth, y'all will get a whuppin'."

"Everybody with me?" he asked. Somebody gives him an "amen," and Justin celebrated the "one faithful Baptist on the front row."

I wish I could have asked Justin about his frequent references to hell: a subject unmentioned in Methodist sermons for decades, even in Methodist churches less urbane than Buncombe Street. A summary of Justin's numerous sermons on the place of perdition: Death is God's punishment for our sin. Hell is a real place that's often referenced in Scripture. Hell is horrible, though we shouldn't blame God for creating hell and sending nonbelievers straight to it. God has created you able to freely choose whether or not to go to hell. The choice is yours. If you find yourself in hell, you've got nobody to blame but yourself and your lousy exercise of God's gift of your free will.

In all this, Justin allows his Baptist inclinations to get the best of his incipient Wesleyanism.

August 4, 2024, Justin preached from 2 Thessalonians 1, focusing exclusively on verse 9: "They will pay the penalty of eternal destruction away from the Lord's presence and away from his mighty glory," assuming that Paul was giving the Thessalonians hell.

"Have you ever felt that you were under spiritual attack? I felt that way this morning when I didn't want to get out of bed and come to church and preach this message that had been laid upon me by God. I prayed, 'Lord, give me grace, give me strength.'"

"The notion that there is a place where we are eternally separated from God and God allows it is an uncomfortable thought. The reality is that the Bible has a lot to say about it and the reality is that a lot of churches won't even talk about it." "Hell is the forgotten doctrine of the church."

Justin lamented, "Hell has been popularized by Halloween and Hollywood" when it's not funny. We ought never "tell someone to go to hell or give them the bird . . . we should take it very serious. We should never celebrate Halloween. You can do what you want, but I'm just tellin' you. . . ." Barely audible nervous laughter was heard in the congregation.

Venturing even further afield from 2 Thessalonians, Justin asserted that "Jesus came so that we could be saved from the wrath of God." "God is a God of judgment." "Hell was created because he is just and good." God doesn't "send people to hell," "sin sends people to hell." "Hell is reserved for those who don't seek salvation. There, they will be eternally tormented."

To bolster his advocacy for hell, Justin cited Jesus's parable of Lazarus and the rich man in hell (Luke 16:19-31). Oops. Jesus's parable puts only the wealthy in hell, though Justin knows that few Buncombe Street hearts would rise to the notion that their riches might hasten them toward eternal torment.

Personal wealth went unmentioned. "How do we avoid hell? By grace through faith in Jesus Christ. Confess your sin. Make a decision for Christ. Now. He is the only one who can keep us from hell, from the wrath of God." "It's our job to take this message into the world."

I'm not bothered that no sermon like this has been preached in the two centuries of Buncombe Street, but I'm baffled by this hammering on hell, even if Paul and Luke didn't, particularly in the context of Buncombe Street Methodist. Justin's colloquial, down-home-aw-shucks, I'm just tellin' you, y'all ever think about that? folksiness appears to have served him well. He beguilingly delivered a sermon in which he portrayed himself as a courageous spokesman for the Bible, telling us things no Methodist preacher had the guts to say and apparently his listeners love it or look the other way.

The sermon closed with a predictable appeal. Accept Jesus, and so forth. On the video, I couldn't see that anybody did. The next week, in my phone interviews with people at Buncombe Street, I asked if they agreed with the assertions Justin made in this sermon. Couldn't find anyone who shared his views on the unquenchable wrath of God or the menace of Halloween, though all said, "We love Justin. He preaches the Bible."

I decided that Emily's sweet, soothing, praise music, heard by The Table congregants, softened the blow of Justin's assertions from the stage. Though it felt like Justin often tried to cut through the warm, gracious glow engendered by the musicians, the music made a greater emotional impact than his sermons. Justin's rational, direct arguments were no match for the emotional clout of the music.

November 6, 2022, Sunday after the vote, All Saints, rather than take a victory lap with the disaffiliates, Justin returned to a favorite theme: "Do you wanna come talk to me if you don't believe in hell? Let's sit down and go through the Bible together. The Bible talks a lot about hell." [Hell is mentioned a mere fifty-four times in the old King James, and in only a few of those passages is "hell" a place of eternal torment. In many cases, "hell" is an inexact translation by the Authorized Version.]

Digression: John Wesley made an attempt to sort out the various words used for what's translated as "hell" in the KJV. Wesley came up with six different places where souls might relocate after death. Sermon 73, "Of Hell."

Wesley speculated that a few, a very few, actually attained sinless perfection in this life, earning them immediate access to paradise. (Calvinists and Lutherans loathed such Wesleyan sanctificationist, perfectionist speculation.) For the rest of us, Wesley said we go first to Hades (aka Sheol, "the Pit"), which has two departments: paradise (for the good), Gehenna (for the bad). Wesley said that's where the thief on the cross landed (Luke 23:43). All saved people (including babies as well as righteous people who never got a chance to hear about Jesus) go to paradise to await final judgment. Those who are not saved or who may have been saved but have backslid go to Gehenna, a kinder, gentler version of hell. Bad, but not yet everlasting torment. Real hell comes only after the final judgment when souls from Gehenna and paradise are raised and judged, the good ones off to heaven, the Gehenna crowd to hell where they will suffer in agony forever. Oh yes, don't forget Tartarus, a place of ultra torment for Satan and his fallen angels.

Never heard of Sermon 73? Good. A rare instance of Wesley indulging in vain theological speculation, a warning to us with lesser minds not to let our sermons go to hell. Understand why none of this ended up in Wesley's Fifty-two Sermons and is only briefly alluded to in his Notes on the New Testament? Wesley knew that there were ten times more passages on the evils of riches than on all the words translated as "hell."

I, like Justin, heard only a rumor of hell in my formative years at Buncombe Street. The first Bible verse I learned by heart was not 2 Thessalonians 1:9, but John 3:16, earning me fifty cents from Mr. Sanders, my third year in the Primary Sunday School Class. "God so loved. . . ."

Here's a kind, loving passage that Wesley adored:

When God our savior's kindness and love appeared, he saved us because of his mercy, not because of righteous things we had done. He did it through the washing of new birth and the renewing by the Holy Spirit, which God poured out upon us generously through Jesus Christ our savior. (Titus 3:4-6)

The peculiar way that Jesus saves is not by getting us to heroically make wise choices but rather by Christ's adoption of us into his family, the church. Salvation is a group thing, Buncombe Street, God taking us as a crowd, many of whom are not my type:

After this I looked, and there was a great crowd that no one could number. They were from every nation, tribe, people, and language. They were standing before the throne and before the Lamb. They wore white robes and held palm branches in their hands. They cried out with a loud voice:

"Victory belongs to our God
who sits on the throne,
and to the Lamb." (Rev 7:9-10)

Our vaunted decisions don't determine our relationship with Christ. In Jesus Christ, God has decided for us. Not waiting for us to come to our senses and ask to be saved, Jesus sought us out for salvage. What did Jesus do as he lay three days in the tomb? First Peter says that he went to hell and preached to all who had never heard of him (1 Pet 3:19); Jesus is nothing if not salvific.

A. V. Huff, retired professor and UMC elder, told me a wild story, from his miserable time as a token member of the Way Forward committee, when a church trustee, trembling with rage, said that The UMC had sunk so low as to teach that Jesus "went to hell." A. V. produced a Bible and read to him 1 Peter 3:19, maybe even the creeds, Apostle's and Nicaean, for all I know. A. V.'s me-love-Bible-better-than-you accuser, devotee of a defrocked preacher in Texas, remained unmoved.

A major reason why a nice person like Jesus ended up on a cross was not to satisfy a holy God but because he saved the wrong people,

people whom nobody thought could be saved, those whom nobody wanted saved. Jesus didn't ask those sinners to make a public declaration of orthodox faith. What he asked was for sinners to let themselves be loved, to risk turnaround from the way they were headed, let go of their self-concern and self-righteousness, and "follow me." Jesus, sounding like a Wesleyan.

Still, I must admit that if you ask Buncombe Street's oldtimers, "What is the gospel?" you'll probably hear good old mainline liberalism: "Jesus is an example for us. He loved everyone, especially children and people with disabilities, and judged nobody. We ought to live that way too, working for peace with justice, building the kingdom of God right here in Greenville. Diverse. Inclusive. Affirming. Oh yes, and please, try hard to be nice."

Maybe Justin's hellfire-and-brimstone sermons received such a positive hearing at The Table because some people had tired of saccharine Methodist schmaltz.

One thing that set Justin apart from us run-of-the-mill Methodists was his delight in preaching from the Old Testament, courageously subjecting his listeners to series on Jeremiah, Ezekiel, Nehemiah (nine weeks in 2023). Even Leviticus, telling the congregation, "I hope to make Leviticus your favorite book of the Bible!" His enthusiasm for Scripture was apparent and contagious.

With a hearty, "You don't hear much talk about this in the Methodist Church, but you are gonna hear it now," Justin dove into obscure Hebrew Scripture, guiding his congregation through *terra incognita*, reading the Old Testament through the lens of Christ, though with a severely truncated Christology, Christ honed down to an agent of substitutionary atonement.

Rarely did he go deeply into a text or listen for its unique voice. He thematically piled biblical passages on top of themselves, ignoring a given text's particular witness or anything in the text that might be counter to his theological preconceptions.

Preaching on Leviticus, Justin launched into a polemic against Torah, the laws of God to Israel, ridiculing those who futilely tried to follow Levitical law. "That's why we have Jesus," Justin explains. "Without Jesus, we are damned."

Due to this sort of preaching, many of Justin's critics dismissed him as "Baptist." No, he's a latter-day John Piper–inflected Calvinist.

Excursus: I defended Buncombe Street Arminianism by playing church basketball against neo-Calvinist Piper, though Piper claims no memory of our adolescent encounters on the court. His dad was pastor of a Baptist church in a Greenville mill village. Piper was better at basketball than he is at theology. Though I was sixteen at the time, if memory serves me, Piper was just as gloomy a Calvinistic complementarian back then as now.

To John Calvin we owe the notion (originating in Anselm) that the heart of Christian proclamation is that Jesus is here chiefly to suffer in order to expiate God's wrath that eternally consigns some to heaven, some to hell.

Justin's sermon on August 14, 2022, argued that Isaiah is "a prophet of judgment." While "the God of the Old Testament is the same God that we see in Jesus," God never got over a nasty tendency to judge and punish, so God sent Jesus to be our proxy in meeting God's just, holy, though impossible standards. In other words, Jesus rescues us from God.

Then Justin veered from Isaiah: "When I read about Judah, I think about America. . . . I come from a patriotic family, I am not knocking America, . . . the problem is with all of this sin."

"My family watches *Hee Haw* reruns and *The Sound of Music* and realize how dirty TV has become. I think America's in deep. . . . I can't say that in church."

"The Bible says that you have to repent before you can come to God. What Isaiah is saying is that God says when we don't repent, he will wash his hands of us. . . . I grew up in The United Methodist Church where grace is preached. I appreciate that, but we could use a little more judgment!" Isaiah is "about judgment, judgment, judgment. . . . Don't tell me that God is not an angry, judgmental God. He was in the Old Testament. He is in the New, but he sent Jesus."

"I'm a Christian first, and then I have my politics. . . . I don't let the media tell me how to be a Christian. The Bible says it, Israel is the chosen nation, if you read the New Testament, you will see that now we, believers, are the chosen," background accompaniment for the Disaffiliation Task Force meeting the coming week.

Justin rarely mentioned contemporary events. January 10, 2021, the Sunday after the insurrection on the U.S. Capitol, Justin just said, "The day all the stuff has happened at the Capitol felt like I was living in a crazy world." "We need the Lord." Then Justin gave thanks that God gives us Sunday worship for "recharging."

"Everybody gets tense when I talk about the culture, but in so many ways, our culture resembles the failure of Israel during Jeremiah's day." It's been a bad thirty years. Evidence? "When I go to the gym, you see ladies walking around, showing their whole belly in a halter top. Somebody would come in from thirty years ago and say, 'Why is everybody walking around in their undergarments?'"

In February 2019, there was a culture clash when a sixteen-year-old member of Buncombe Street returned from the church's annual "Walk with Christ" retreat, sort of like a Walk to Emmaus for youth. Tad stood before the congregation at The Table and said that he felt such love and acceptance on the retreat that now he was able to declare before the church that he was "nonbinary."

Witnesses are divided on what happened next except that Justin chastised Tad. "We don't believe that." "Genesis says God created us male and female."

The video has been removed from the web.

The next Sunday Justin reported that some members of the church felt he didn't say clearly enough that gay is sin. A big sin.

Then there was December 4, 2022, Second Sunday of Advent, when Justin went full throttle, Travelers Rest post-tribulationist, postmillennialist. "We're gonna talk about something today that I've never heard talked about. . . . the rapture. When I say 'rapture,' I know that's a trigger word. . . . the *Left Behind* series. . . . The rapture says that when Jesus returns, he will take the believers, and he will separate them from the nonbelievers. The believers will actually be taken to heaven. . . . I didn't have exposure to this when I was growing up, nobody taught me about this. I just went to church and we had a feel-good message. We didn't actually talk about what the Bible says. . . . It's really weird to me because the foundation of our denomination was on preaching about judgment, and hell. . . . All we hear about today is the goodness and mercy. Well, you can't heal the church if you don't preach about hell. Just like a doctor cannot cure cancer if the doctor don't talk about cancer. . . . Hell is what Jesus came to save us from. . . . We need to talk about what the Bible actually says."

Excursus: "What the Bible actually says" was the one phrase from this rapture diatribe that may have been preached at Buncombe Street a century ago. It was the foundation for the white Southern defense of slavery. If the Bible says "slaves," it's okay to enslave.

Dear Dr. Moseley, in his *Buncombe Street Story*, says that in the 1830s, "The little Greenville Methodist Church would find itself reflecting the tenor of those years. Within its sanctuary and its balconies would mingle master and slave. From its pulpit would thunder forth 'scriptural truth' for the upholding of impossible ideas and institutions. . . ."

In other words, in the church eventually named Buncombe Street, built upon land gifted by the state's largest slaveholder, master and slave heard "scriptural truth," claiming that because the Bible actually says slavery, enslavement is established by the Word of God. Biblical fundamentalism and literalism were thus born.

Justin continued, "There will be a separation," and that's the rapture. "If you knew a thief was coming in the night to your house, you would be sitting there in the corner with your shotgun, right? I believe that the enemy is sitting out there in the woods, watching us, ready to jump. And we're going around like he didn't exist."

While Justin was preaching the rapture at The Table, senior pastor Brian Gilmer preached Luke 2 at the traditional service, John's "baptism of repentance." Preaching engagingly, and without notes, Brian says that we need to prepare for Christmas during Advent by looking for "what is good and holy."

"Are the preparations we make each year for Advent and Christmas enough?" We "fall out of step with who God has called us to be." In short, we need to repent, which Brian described as turning around and "living the lives we should." "We need to ask for the . . . unmerited grace of God."

In my few conversations with folks who attended The Table, all expressed love and affection for Justin. But then I reminded them that "Justin says that if you don't publicly confess your sin and Jesus Christ as Lord and accept him as your Savior, then God will consign you to eternal punishment in hell," or "Say you are driving down Wade Hampton Boulevard and the rapture occurs. Because you have publicly confessed Jesus, you get raptured up to heaven. Your spouse hasn't, sending them straight to hell. Right?" "How about Halloween costumes?"

Their chief response: "I'm not sure about all that. But I do admire Justin for standing up for what he believes and preaching the Bible."

In short, I sensed a disconnect between Justin's preaching and his congregation. His listeners gratefully related to his public personality, his humility and smile, and the colloquial, enthusiastic style in which his sermons were delivered rather than to the Scripture he preached. Never once, in all my interviews with those at Open Hearts, did anyone express anger or resentment against Justin. Justin's personality overcame any of his listeners' possible misgivings about his what-the-Bible-says sermons.

I was thus surprised to hear a young congregant say, "I don't think Justin likes us," citing Justin's joshing of his listeners' lack of biblical knowledge and unresponsiveness during his sermons. "Would it kill you to say 'Amen'?" and "Let's see the hands . . . oh well." He criticized the folks at The Table for their inattention to regular early morning Bible study, for being known around town "for what we're against" rather than "what we are for," their spiritual contentedness, failure to pray, and their miserly stewardship. "I've been trying for ten years to get you to say

'Amen.'" He joshes, "Y'all are getting on my nerves. I'm tryn' to get you fired up but it ain't happening."

In his March 27, 2022, sermon Justin scolded, "This isn't a country club." The congregation's uneasiness was palpable, even on the video. "This is a hospital for broken people." Perhaps sensing that he had overstepped, he added, "For the most part, y'all are doing a really great job. I just want us to get better."

I think Justin saw himself as attempting to change the culture of the staid, establishment, self-satisfied, middle-of-the-road church that he inherited. He wanted a more faithful Buncombe Street. Behind Justin's "Don't mean to beat up on you but . . ." is a demanding view of church. Single-handedly, working exclusively from the pulpit, Justin was attempting what few Methodist preachers have: transformation of a historic, downtown, self-satisfied congregation.

While questioning Justin's biblical interpretation, I have to ask, just how "biblical" was the preaching I heard growing up at Buncombe Street? Not much. How often did a preacher confront us with our tepid commitment to Christ? Rarely. How many opportunities were we given to boldly step forward and pray or risk participation in mission or verbally, publicly sign on with Jesus? How come we never heard about Jesus's apocalyptic threats?

We just weren't that sort of church.

I'll admit it. Justin's preaching challenges my own. Am I envious that Justin's preaching is better appreciated, at least at Buncombe Street, than mine? Wish my personality were so pleasing that my listeners would say, "Not sure about that sermon, but who cares? He's really, really likable."

And how has my preaching been in rebellion against the sermons that I grew up with at Buncombe Street, even as Justin rebels against the preaching he heard as a student at Duke Divinity? Is Justin's the homiletics of the future?

My first churchy book was *The Gospel for the Person Who Has Everything*. Though unintended, that book could be read as a critique of the flaccid, middle-of-the-road-muddling-Methodist preaching I grew up hearing at Buncombe Street. Justin and I both enjoy narrating our lives as a series of conversions and repentings from the faith we each were handed. In what ways does our rebellion hinder our hearing what Scripture wants to say to the church today? Wish I could have had that preacher-to-preacher conversation.

Justin began the new year, January 7, 2024, opening his sermon by connecting with the congregation's new mission statement to "Engage, equip, and empower." "Everything we do in the church has got to be held up against the question 'is it developing a follower of Jesus Christ'?" "We are not a country club, we are not a social justice club, we are a group of people who make disciples for Jesus," rummaging about the New Testament for proof texts.

Then Justin produced a chainsaw. Calling a young girl down front, he acted as if he was equipping her to use the saw. Get it? We need to be equipped as followers of Jesus.

While we live in an age "when the culture is changing and shifting, and going in an opposite direction from the church," the new Buncombe Street is "rooted in the word, fed by the truth." We've got ourselves a new symbol: the United Methodist Cross and Flame has been supplanted by a cross and an open Bible, though I don't see how that's related to the nonbiblical mission statement.

Justin's claim that the new Buncombe Street embodies the fresh mission statement is aspirational at best. The Buncombe Street—"my" church—that Justin inherited, was established, institutionalized, mainline Protestant liberalism, with a vague, civic orientation, in which the gospel had been demythologized, subjectivized, individualized, psychologized, and sentimentalized with a Southern accent. Justin and his inner circle of advocates convinced themselves that now at last they were hearing pure, unadulterated Bible preached. "Y'all, it may make you uncomfortable, but this is just what the Bible says." In truth, the gospel they're hearing is as culturally compromised as the genteel, neighborly, culturally accommodated, innocuous gospel on which I was raised, just in different ways.

I'm sorry, I can't see the connection between the new Buncombe Street's vision statement and biblical authority. "Equipping, engaging, empowering disciples" is a stock-and-trade United Methodist sort of slogan. No mention of salvation, making a decision for Christ, biblical authority, death, the Second Coming, brokenness, or hell, all fixations of sermons at The Table.

The September 29, 2024 "Community Newsletter" of the new Buncombe Street bragged about the men's ministry, Kairos Prison Ministry, basketball registration, Fall Tailgate, Safe Sanctuary Training, Dominican Republic Youth Mission Trip, Operation Christmas Child, B-Street Students; the typical, well-functioning, full-program mainline United Methodist church that I always wanted to create; nothing independent or new there.

In late fall 2024, Buncombe Street advertised for a pastor of discipleship. No seminary training or MDiv, no denominational relationship required. Okay. But there's but one reference to Jesus, and none to Scripture or salvation in the job description; no mention of any of the chief assertions that led Buncombe Street to disaffiliate.

God help me, when I hear "salvation," I think not of Anselm, Calvin, or "biblical authority" but of my teacher in the Primary Division Sunday school. I don't remember her name but I still see her there, with the camellia pinned to her bodice.

The summit of her long career as children's Sunday school teacher had to be her beloved annual performance of Daniel 3. Three young men, "not much older than you," with improbable names, cast by the evil king who had an even odder name, into the fiery furnace. "The furnace was seven times hotter than usual. Hellishly hot. How hot was it? It was so hot that the people who threw the three young men into the furnace got burned to a crisp, just throwing them in."

Geeze, that's hot. I already knew how it all ended, prepped by my mother's breakfast reading from *Hurlbut's Story of the Bible*. But oh how well Miss What's-Her-Name knew her craft. She paused for effect to allow us innocents to relish the horror, the heat, the smell, and the smoke (knowing we were all born South Carolina violent). Then she asked, "Where is God in this story of horrible Nebuchadnezzar and his fiery furnace?"

God? Don't recall God making it into the story. No hands raised.

Looking us straight in the eye, she whispered conspiratorially, "The king looked into the furnace. And behold, Nebuchadnezzar saw therein, four, not three. Just walking in the flames. Unscathed. Four!

"Boys and girls, what does this mean?"

We give up. You tell us, said we by our stupefied silence.

"There is nowhere you go, God won't go looking . . . looking for you," pointing to each of us, "and you, and you, in order for God to walk with you," she decreed triumphantly. "Even as God walked with Adam and Eve in the cool of the garden, or with Isaac and Abraham up Mount Moriah, as Jesus journeyed with his disciples on the way to Emmaus, or appeared to Saul on the Damascus Road," her bird-like voice shrilling in crescendo, "God walks with you. Even in the furnace. God refuses to leave your side. The flames are no hindrance. Jesus said it, showed it; God covets . . . you. And God always gets what God desires. *You.*

"Now, let's have our closing prayer so you may join your parents for church."

Forty years later, Sunday afternoon, Duke Chapel, when a tardy Desmond Tutu at last burst through the chapel's gothic front door and strode down the aisle to thunderous applause, Channel 11 cameras, spotlights, at the very moment we were whooping, "When through fiery trials thy pathways shall lie, my grace, all sufficient shall be thy supply. . . ."

I stood atop of the chancel steps, embraced Bishop Tutu, and showed him the way to the chapel's pulpit. Though it was the grandest moment of my days at Duke, my heart was elsewhere: an ancient woman adorned with pink camellia, in the upstairs Primary Room at Buncombe Street, going about the job assigned by her church, a church that loved its young enough to commission her to tell us the truth, the whole truth, and nothing but the truth about God.

Jesus saves.

Trinity/Open Hearts

August 2024, a year and a half after formal disaffiliation, leaders, clergy and lay, of the new, independent Buncombe Street Methodist Church had cause for celebration:

Dear Church Family and Friends,

It has been a great summer at Buncombe Street! . . . Vacation Bible School. . . . B-Street Kids just returned from a heart-changing trip to Asbury Hills at Camp Moseley. Mission trip teams traveled to Ecuador and Costa Rica. . . . In June, we had a sermon series focused on invitation, and we encouraged you to host (or attend) a summer gathering for fellowship and to grow our church community. . . . Twenty nine (29) new members joined Buncombe Street this summer, and . . . with over 800 attending Sunday worship, we are similar to pre-pandemic attendance. . . . When we disaffiliated from the UMC last year, we defaulted to an independent church. . . . This fall we will explore our options of a denominational alignment or remaining independent. . . . As of June 30, 2024, we have $1,377,086 given towards Operations . . . a shortfall of $95,614. We have received $98,004 towards Missions & Outreach so far this year, leaving $151,996 still needed. . . . Our Next Chapter fund represents our loan from disaffiliation from the United Methodist Church in 2023. We have paid off $2,042,754; however, our outstanding loan balance is $1,157,246. . . .

God has been at work at our church and great things lie ahead at Buncombe Street. . . .

To God be the Glory,

Justin Gilreath

Senior Pastor

Krista Bannister

Church Council Chair

May the God of endurance and encouragement grant you to live in such harmony with one another, in accord with Christ Jesus, that together you may with one voice glorify the God and Father of our Lord Jesus Christ. Therefore welcome one another as Christ has welcomed you, for the glory of God.

Romans 15:5-7 [ESV]

Also impressive, in differing ways, was the new church happening across town at 2703 Augusta Street. Karen Jones was regathering the flock at Trinity, those who had stuck with struggling Trinity through the thick and thin of their botched adoption, a few hundred UMC loyalist refugees from the new Buncombe Street, and a slowly growing group of newcomers looking for a church trying to be half as welcoming as Jesus.

Designated by the S.C. Conference as a new UMC church plant, a huge task lay before them. Many in the congregation felt battered and hurt by the leadership of Buncombe Street, not only by their willingness—in some cases even eagerness—to see them go, but also by Buncombe Street's neglect of Trinity's building, the selling of Trinity's beloved retreat center at Junaluska, and the stripping of Trinity's few assets. On top of that, Buncombe Street had been allowed to exit The UMC with credit given for every dime it spent on Trinity over the years, thus lessening the amount of money paid for Buncombe Street's separation. This meant that Trinity's new church start would probably get less conference support since the *Discipline* directed that money received from disaffiliations was to go toward church planting in nearby urban areas.

In a determined demonstration of resurrection, Trinity was renamed "Open Hearts UMC," signifying the new, unbolted, loyally, gratefully

Wesleyan congregation they aspired to be. "Open" is an inadequate adjective for Christian believing and action, and I'm suspicious of sentimental "heart" talk (used ubiquitously, you may recall, by the DS to control and distract Buncombe Street's April 2023 "discernment" meeting). "Open" and "heart" are put under suspicion by Christian theology. Historically, Christians have sought to speak from Scripture rather than from the notoriously self-deceitful human heart. And no Christian is supposed to say "I believe that Jesus Christ is Lord, but I am open to consideration of other Saviors if you have one more appealing and less demanding." Still, we're all grateful that Trinity didn't rename itself "2703 Augusta Street United Methodist Church."

Above all, I agree with Justin when he said in a sermon that it's better for a church to be known for what it's for rather than what it's against. Therefore, I'm glad to see "Open Hearts" beginning a story about the vibrant embrace and reiteration of Wesleyan Christianity in Greenville.

As Karen Jones told a reporter, "What unifies our congregation is our common passion to love God and serve our neighbors with our hearts, minds and strength. My hope is that we will be a church that serves as a brave space for all people seeking to deepen their relationship with Jesus Christ through study, worship, and service, where we can have differing opinions and still respect and love each other as God commands."[3]

The narrative of Buncombe Street is a cautionary tale showing that connectional, itinerating, evangelical Methodism is a demanding polity requiring constant refurbishment and inculcation. BSUMC paid dearly for its history of neglecting the formation and integration of new members into Wesleyanism. It was easier to attract Baptist, neo-Calvinist, congregationalists and give them a Methodist shine, clustering around what's left of the conservative faith they've inhaled just by living in Greenville than to venture church the Wesleyan way.

Buncombe Street's story is inescapably a tragedy, no matter how positive a spin you put on it. I interviewed a dozen former members of

3. "New United Methodist Church plant opens to serve the faith needs of the Greenville community," *Greenville News*, December 19, 2023, https://whosonthemove.com/new-united-methodist-church-plant-opens-to-serve-the-faith-needs-of-the-greenville-community/.

Buncombe Street who are now either reluctantly Presbyterian, Episcopalian, or vow never to enter any church ever again. Anybody who claims that Buncombe Street's disaffiliation was amicable should talk to them. Any bishop who tries to narrate this story with a happy ending needs to reckon with those who, because of their experience of what went down at my home church, are lost forever to the church, any church.

But there are also those at this new church start who are trying, by the grace of God, to move beyond the tragic. Among some at Open Hearts there's pain and anger, yes. But there's also inspiring, positive embrace of the power of United Methodist itinerant, connectional, accountable, truly evangelical, episcopal polity. This is quite remarkable since, as we have seen, the refugees who left Buncombe Street were not that well served by UMC overseers.

At the beginning, I thought I would tell the story of those grieving the loss of Buncombe Street. But I soon found that many at Open Hearts weren't grieving; they were gratefully celebrating a new church plant that's trying to move positively into whatever future God has for them, attempting to boldly reach out to whomever Jesus Christ invites to his table:

"I can breathe again now that I'm out of that toxic church environment."

"Frankly, I'm glad not to have any responsibility for that big, expensive, corporation—that nobody knows how to run—called Buncombe Street."

"It's good to go to a church where I don't have to fear that the preacher will say something hurtful about people I love."

"I'm not a refugee; I'm part of something new that's better than the old."

"People at Open Hearts are not here to see and be seen. I love that."

"I'm glad to be in a church where people ask, 'How can we welcome you?' rather than, 'Whose side are you on?'"

Open Hearts is doing more than putting a happy face on a sad situation. They are rediscovering the wonder of a redemptive Savior who delights at befriending the omitted, revivifying the dead, healing the broken, and making a way when we thought there was none. Things keep dying in Christianity, but keep rising again due to Jesus, the only one who knows the way out of the grave. How he loves to show off by raising corpses, binding up the wounded, and welcoming those who thought they were excluded, this time on Augusta Street in Greenville.

Still, there's pain. No one who had left to be at Open Hearts reported having had any of the Buncombe Street clergy say simply, "Sorry to see you go." Les Pritchard did try to talk one into staying with, "Surely you don't want a church where you might get a homosexual as a pastor." A couple told me that Grover refuses to speak to them when they see him in town.

"Those who stayed were glad to see us go so they could at last have a church where nobody dared question Baptist biblical interpretation," groused another.

And yet, Open Hearts is doing better than making the best of a painful loss; they could be the future of Methodism. I have been roving about the face of the earth, telling ailing congregations, "In the present moment, every United Methodist church ought to consider itself a new church start. Don't rest on your past; go ahead, don't look back, risk a major reset. United Methodism can be a gift to so many; get out there and share it." That's what they are already trying to do at Open Hearts.

First Sunday of December, 2024, while Janice apocalyptically threatened, but gently, independent Buncombe Street, Karen preached enthusiastically, downright evangelistically to Open Hearts from Luke 21. "What a harsh, dark text to begin Advent," she acknowledged. "But let's not run away from it," she said, "let's run toward it." With help from Barbara Brown Taylor's book *Learning to Walk in the Dark*, Karen allowed Luke to coax her into preaching Christ's Advent, not as somber threat, but as joyful divine redemption drawing near.

O Bible-believing disaffiliates at Buncombe Street, who's being biblical now?

The new Buncombe Street is not all that new. I can't imagine that it has much of a future if all it tries to be is another all-white, mainline Protestant, free-church, low-church congregation that brags about being more closed and conservative than those lax Episcopalians across town.

But maybe their brand of fearful conservatism is what most people are in the market for these days.

I, like Justin, think Buncombe Street Church could be so much more.

Open Hearts is also less new than it will need to be. For all of their claims to be a fresh expression of Methodism in Greenville, Open Hearts looks to me like a typical UMC: conventional Colonial Revival, expensive-to-maintain building, high-median-age congregation, children's sermon, periodic Communion, aging choir, traditional music (finally, the organ has been fixed), with warm, gracious, though sometimes bordering-on-sentimental messages.

I found Karen Jones's preaching to be steadfastly, carefully biblical, lectionary based, well-prepared and thoughtful but with a hospitable, upbeat, ingratiating tone. Just like Justin, Karen frequently shares insights from her biblical study with the congregation, and she enjoys the Old Testament almost as much, but for very different reasons. The theme of a loving God who expects us to love too always comes through.

On October 20, 2024, Karen preached a vibrantly biblical sermon on Galatians 3, giving encouragement and christological justification for the church Open Hearts means to be. Here, we'll have unity and togetherness for no reason other than Jesus has convened us. I wish Karen's christological sermon could have been preached at Buncombe Street a couple of years ago, but as I've admitted, maybe truly biblical preaching doesn't have as great an impact upon a congregation as Justin and I hoped.

Here's how Open Hearts describes themselves:

We are a new congregation that is proud to be a part of the United Methodist denomination and we strive to embody the values of open hearts, open minds, and open doors. We believe that by opening ourselves to others, we can create a welcoming and inclusive community where everyone can feel valued and supported. We recognize that faith is a journey, and we embrace the diversity of perspectives and backgrounds that make up our congregation. Our community is a place where you can ask questions, share your experiences, and learn from one another in an atmosphere of warmth and acceptance.

We believe that being a good neighbor is at the heart of our faith, and we strive to extend kindness and compassion to everyone we encounter. Through our worship, outreach, and service activities, we hope to spread the message of God's love in our community and beyond. We encourage you to stop by and get to know us—we look forward to getting to know you as well!

I don't know why Jesus isn't mentioned in the Open Hearts welcome, maybe because The UMC stock phrase, "open minds, open hearts, open doors," doesn't adequately encapsulate the good news Christ preached or enacted. "Welcoming and inclusive community" seems to be how they define what Scripture calls body of Christ, but that's just my guess.

Judging from the appearance of Open Hearts, their claim to be an "inclusive community" is, as yet, aspirational. Still, it's a worthy biblical, evangelical ambition. At least they're trying to catch up with Jesus.

"Faith is a journey," "we embrace a diversity of perspectives," "a place where you can ask questions, share your experiences" bathed in "warmth and acceptance" and the gospel summed up as "the message of God's love," good old mainline prosaicisms. Not much fresh or new. Maybe these timeworn liberal platitudes are Open Hearts' protest against new Buncombe Street's determined lack of diversity and warmth, but I'm not sure these clichés are substantial enough to beckon Open Hearts where they want to go.

As is the case for the future of all congregations, God only knows.

Tomorrow

"We don't have a permanent city here, but rather we are looking for the city that is still to come" (Heb 13:14). That's the text Bishop Tullis preached at my ordination on a hot, June Sunday night in Clinton, South Carolina, at Broad Street UMC. (What makes Methodists name our churches for streets?) My mother's Aldersgate Sunday School Class (revered, though feared by our clergy) sent me a genuine leather toiletries kit, stamped with my name in gold in celebration of my chirotony. Though I was grateful, I told Mother it seemed an odd ordination gift. She snapped back, "Not for one who vows to go wherever the church sticks him."

The bishop's Hebrews text seemed equally odd for the ordination of a twenty-six-year-old. Why should I need reminding of ministry's impermanence? Maybe Bishop Tullis thought that Hebrews 13:14 is a truth to be laid upon novices: Hey kid, only God has a future. Nothing human is built to last. Legacies are a delusion. Jesus is the Savior of the world, not you. Work hard, do your best, but always remember that we, our creations, including our churches, are impermanent. God not only makes alive but also kills (Deut 32:39). Here we have no everlasting city. With a resurrecting God, keep the present church in your rearview mirror as you look down the street for the bride of Christ's unpredictable arrival.

When the loyal UMs at Buncombe Street named their committee "Save Our Legacy," clinging to what they had from the past rather than reaching toward God's future, Hebrews 13:14 implies they were doomed. Only God's love is steadfast. Legacies are God's self-assignment, not ours.

One of my seminarians served as a summer intern at Buncombe Street. He wrote, "To my surprise, there's your framed picture. Archives Room, only space they had free to serve as my office. Didn't know this was your home church. Nobody else does either. Only the archivist remembers you. Sorry."

Jesus, you have so many ways of reminding preachers of our frailty, vulnerability, corrigibility, contingency, and impermanence. As Paul said, "We have this treasure in clay pots so that the awesome power belongs to God and doesn't come from us. . . . We always carry Jesus' death around in our bodies so that Jesus' life can also be seen in our bodies. We who are alive are always being handed over to death for Jesus' sake" (2 Cor 4:7-11).

How I loved standing before Duke undergrads, first week of Lent, looking upon their youthfulness, and smearing ashes on their foreheads, telling an Ash Wednesday truth this culture dodges: "Remember that you are dust and to dust you shall return." In writing this book, I've learned that it's more fun to smear ashes on someone else's forehead than to have them imposed on you.

I know, I know. At my advanced age, my job is to recede, depart, and hand off the church to the kids, vacate the pulpit for the pew, sit with my surviving friends, and complain about the air conditioning, the sound system, and the Cream of Wheat being ladled from the pulpit. New independent Buncombe Street, go on ahead without me.

As I depart a church that's yours and won't stay mine, Open Hearts, I hand off to you the beloved, but now considerably diminished UMC that I bore. No, it's not my church or yours. It's God's. Our only hope: that Christ will bear his beloved body into the future, no matter how badly we've abused it.

When he addressed General Conference in Charlotte (April 24, 2024) as spokesperson for the Council of Bishops, Bishop Holston repetitiously shouted that The UMC should grit its teeth, strengthen its resolve, stop licking its wounds, forget the goof-ups of the past two years, disaffiliation and all that, and become what "God needs us to be!"

I'm not sure about that theology. Thank God, time and again, God has, despite our screwups, gone on ahead, taken the church in hand, and been God anyway, regardless of us. Tomorrow's church is whatever God does with it. May it more closely resemble the bride of Christ than the church I received, labored to bear, vainly tried to lead, and much of it, lost. Only God has a future. Our only hope is that Christ will hitch his poor old compromised church onto whatever tomorrow God's got in mind.

What thinks Jesus of this story that I've told about my home church? It's hard to imagine that he's pleased any time his body is torn. He hates divorce. Malachi 2:16. His mission is always to convene, assemble, seek, reconcile, and save, until he retrieves and ingathers all that's lost. No lamb left behind. Closed doors mean nothing to him. He refuses to let us do church any way we please. What cares he for our balloting? He doesn't leave up to us the final verdict on us.

I believe what the Bible says, and what Buncombe Street taught me about the Trinity is true. No matter how lawyered-up or slick their publicity, disaffiliates of any age have failed to receive much assistance from Jesus. Separatists, secessionists, segregationists, and schismatics, no matter how hard they've looked, have found little support in anything Jesus said or did, whereas reconcilers, redeemers, conveners, and gatherers are delighted by resurrected Jesus appearing to them and working with them, sometimes in spite of them, for togetherness.

These words, first pronounced to me by my home church, long before I had any idea what they meant, are as true as when the first church sang them:

> The Son is the image of the invisible God,
>   the one who is first over all creation,
> Because all things were created by him:
>   both in the heavens and on the earth,
>   the things that are visible and the things that are invisible.
>   Whether they are thrones or powers,
>   or rulers or authorities,
>   all things were created through him and for him.

He existed before all things,
> and all things are held together in him.

He is the head of the body, the church,

who is the beginning,
> the one who is firstborn from among the dead

> so that he might occupy the first place in everything.

Because all the fullness of God was pleased to live in him,
> and he reconciled all things to himself through him—

> whether things on earth or in the heavens.

> > He brought peace through the blood of his cross.

> > (Col 1:15-20)

The church we bear is the church born and borne by Jesus.

Jesus is beloved for his promise of unburdening: "Come to me, all you who are struggling hard and carrying heavy loads, and I will give you rest. Put on my yoke, and learn from me. I'm gentle and humble. And you will find rest for yourselves. My yoke is easy to bear, and my burden is light" (Matt 11:28-30). Surely Jesus speaks ironically: a heavy load is an exhausting burden; a yoke around the necks of the dumbest of farm animals forces them to walk in the same direction whether they want to or not. His burden is light? His yoke easy?

Check that out with your average overburdened pastor who wears a stole, "the yoke of obedience." The night I was ordained at Broad Street Church, even though I knew little of the actual, empirical church, I felt the weight of dozens of clergy hands laid on my head. When a red stole was put around my neck, it felt downright uncomfortable.

"Never forget that the ones you serve are those for whom Christ died," was all I remember Bishop Tullis reading from the ritual, laying upon me a burden I knew that I was too young to bear.

The way I now read Matthew 11:28-30 is this: Jesus promises to take off our backs the pointless burdens the world lays upon us (a happy church, numerical success, the bishop's blessing, a winning personality, accessible sermons, popularity), in order to lay his peculiar burden upon us. The chief burden we bear, for those who have had hands laid upon our heads, is the church.

The main thing to remember in ministry is that Jesus does not intend for us to bear the church alone. Bad things happen when we preachers think we've got the church on our backs. The "church is of God," according to The UMC's ordination service, quoting from the most ancient clergy-making rituals. I wish those words from the ordinal would have been said to Justin. Jesus has assumed the church as his self-assignment. Only he is capable of birthing a church and bearing it into the future. Christ bears with all Christians, enabling us to bear the church, so that we might bear one another's burdens (Gal 6:2), so that we might bear fruit (John 15:8).

"Get this straight: It's *my* church, not yours," Jesus has repeatedly, pointedly had to tell me over the years. I can't make, nor can the next pastor sent them by the GMC make, Buncombe Street's story turn out right. Only God can do that. Finally, Buncombe Street's future is that of any church: *God only knows.*

I do know that the church soon to be borne by my seminarians must be different from the one I bore. A living, active God makes impossible merely taking up the church as we think we remember it. Yet new leaders can courageously assume the burden of the future church with confidence that it is a burden bestowed by Jesus Christ. He has no intention of allowing us to abuse his body or to arrogantly take up this burden as if it were solely our own.

> He is the head of the body, the church,
>> who is the beginning,
>>> the one who is firstborn from among the dead.
>> (Col 1:18)

A former pastor bellyached, "Buncombe Street loves Buncombe Street more than Jesus." How easily affection for a church slides into idolatry, dancing around the golden calf, clutching the deed to a stable-looking, neocolonial building with a gym as substitute for a risky relationship with a living God on the move. Justin said as much when he slammed his Buncombe Street's edifice complex in more than one sermon last fall.

Maybe what happened at Buncombe Street is just a jealous God kicking over my idols? It's easier to bear an undemanding, pastel-to-beige, culturally aligned, boyhood memory of a church than to embrace the burden of a commandeering, in living color, grownup Jesus with holes in hands and feet and a nasty wound in his side. At least both the conservative Friends and the loyalist Preserve Our Legacy groups, for any of their divergence, tried to love a church that actually is rather than one from which I departed fifty years ago.

At every turn in life's road, the Holy Spirit, Jesus contemporized, pushes God's people to go beyond adoring what God did in the past and ask, "What is Jesus up to here and now?" There is no way to make "all things new" (Rev 21:5) without throwing the furniture around. It's hard to hear when you falsely assumed that the church's furniture was securely bolted to the floor and that church as you have known and benefited from it, will go on and on forever and ever, world without end, Amen.

I do know that, when it comes to loving Jesus, something must be lost in order for anything else to be born. Burdens must be set aside in order to take up the burdens he lays upon us. Nobody has ever followed Jesus without relinquishment of somebody, something, or somewhere. In discipleship, there is gain, yes, but loss as well and the losses may be painful. Ask the first disciples: "Follow me," immediately necessitating the abandonment of nets, family fishing business, legacy, and Daddy too (Matt 4:18-22).

Then there was the time that Jesus compared God to a nocturnal thief who breaks in and rips off your treasure (Matt 24:43). Not the most flattering image of our heavenly Father, even if true to most Christians' experience.

You want to buy my Buncombe Street commemorative plate? I inherited it from my mother but now, after all that's happened, I'll part with it for less than I once invested in it.

Still, a redemptive God delights in taking our mess and working it up into something beautiful. Most of the people at Open Hearts think that's happening to them right now. Some at Open Hearts will need to learn to forgive the injustice worked against them by a small group at the new Buncombe Street. They'll have to pray for freedom from the we-won-you-lost goodbye narrative that the disaffiliates at Buncombe Street tried to impose upon them.

Open Hearts, try hard to learn from and not replicate the flaws, factions, and leadership mistakes that produced sadness at my home church. It's not enough for you to boast of being "inclusive," "open," and "welcoming." "Progressive" is an adjective that's not strong enough to produce *ecclesia*. Keep focusing on Scripture and risk letting God's word make church as difficult as Jesus means it to be. You'll have to do the tough, internal and external truth-telling, and risk-taking required to be a church that's truly engaged in the mission of Jesus Christ if you want to have more tomorrows than your yesterdays.

Jesus would love to help you with all that.

Sunday, November 17, 2024. After saying, "Open Hearts would not be here were it not for Buncombe Street Methodist Church. They are deeply shaken by the loss of Justin Gilreath," Karen Jones offered prayers for Justin's family and for Buncombe Street. Karen movingly beseeched Christ's redemption amid this "complicated tragedy."

The memorial service at The Table's auditorium, November 22, 2024, was something else. A Greenville doctor praised Justin for preaching "the Word of God in simple, direct ways," boasting, "He was a Baptist pastor to a Methodist flock." In a not-too-veiled reference to the issue-that's-not-the-one-issue, the doctor claimed that Justin "loved and accepted everyone but he wouldn't compromise the truth for anyone!" Applause.

Billy Graham and Justin died in the same way, claimed the doctor. They were both exhausted in service to Christ. In his last days, Justin had "unrelenting, recurring pain" that led to "daily depression." "He was a wounded warrior, a suffering servant. . . . Justin Gilreath wore himself out . . . but today he is free. . . . He would want us to live as if we are dying and above all to live for Jesus Christ." As if he were defensive about the manner of Justin's dying, the doctor saw parallels in the deaths of Moses and Justin. "Justin Gilreath took this church through [the wilderness of] the most difficult time this church has faced in its two hundred years of existence. He carried this church on his back," but unlike Moses, "Justin is in the Promised Land." Then he took a guitar and sang a country-and-western gospel song about the death and blood of Jesus.

Had I been there, rather than watching from afar, I hope the pastor in me would have prodded me to respond, to all those in the congregation who suffer from depression or chronic pain, all those young people who might be confused by the mixed messages of the doctor's rant, "No!"

A pastor friend of Justin's from a nearby Baptist church followed. He praised Justin for his happy disposition and his many friends. Then he bore down on the congregation. "Denomination doesn't matter, it's just a personal preference. Sorry, gotta say it." "What matters is, Do you have a relationship with Jesus?" Justin did. "He wasn't perfect," but didn't have to be because he was saved.

Then the pastor talked about suicide. "I know that many of you are asking yourselves, 'Where's Justin now? I want you to know, he is not in hell," citing Scripture that proves that Justin's having been saved settled his eternal destination. For those who have been born again, it doesn't matter how you die or even how you live. Once saved, always saved. "Do you have a personal relationship with Jesus?" asked the preacher, repeatedly urging everyone to "choose for yourself" where you will spend eternity "before it's too late." "Have you made that choice?"

A Greenville mortician, who has been present at a thousand funerals, declared to me, "In all my years, I've never witnessed a funeral like that."

Justin, I discovered, had left directions for his service. No Scripture was read. No Methodists nor anyone on the Buncombe Street staff spoke; the speakers bragged that they were Baptists and, in his heart, Justin was too. The best of the service were the few references praising Justin for being a warm, gifted, effective preacher who loved his family; the worst was the biblical misinterpretation and bungled attempts at soteriology. It was also helpful to hear, though brief, references to Jesus as a redemptive savior.

The Sunday after, November 30, Janice preached with a picture of Justin before her in the pulpit, preaching on John 14, "Let not your hearts be troubled" (KJV). I expected a continuance of mourning for Justin. Instead, Janice preached twentieth-century Darbyism and refitted dispensationalism, but nicely, in a pale imitation of her deceased colleague, explaining that Justin had planned a series on the Second Coming of Christ. You've been warned. Be ready. It's the last days. Christ is coming to judge, to end the world. Advent at the new Buncombe Street.

In the following weeks that led up to Christmas, there were few references to Justin, though church newsletters mentioned his "passing," as if that euphemism was an adequate term for the tragedy that had occurred. After enabling Justin's grieving wife and children to move into the spacious new home Justin had meticulously planned and built on his family's farm, Buncombe Street's leaders were moving on.

Benign Mike Guffey was called back into service, yet again, at last more honestly, openly GMC, to help the new Buncombe Street through its time of bereavement. In his sermon on December 15, Mike preached a bunch of heartwarming stories on the theme of the Incarnation of Christ, the only time I could recall that folks at The Table had heard mention of God's loving enfleshment "for us and our salvation" as the Nicene Creed puts it. Mike's sermon was about as far from Justin's memorial service as a sermon could be.

What should have been preached at the memorial service? *Jesus.* In the end, whether it be a funeral or the dissolution of a church, when there's loss, the church has little to say other than "Jesus saves." During a time of violent turmoil in Israel, cities laid waste, so much looted and lost, Isaiah lifted up his eyes and saw God not only kicking over idols but also making a tomorrow better than the present, neither because Israel had finally gotten serious about biblical authority and honestly repented of sin, nor due to Israel at last being open, inclusive, and affirming but because of who God is and what God is up to:

> Don't you know? Haven't you heard?
>   The LORD is the everlasting God,
>   the creator of the ends of the earth.
>   He doesn't grow tired or weary. . . .
>   Those who hope in the LORD
>   will renew their strength;
>   they will fly up on wings like eagles;
>   they will run and not be tired;
>   they will walk and not be weary. (Isa 40:28, 31)

On January 5, first Sunday of the new year, former senior pastor Jerry Temple was invited back to Buncombe Street, out of retirement (and life in the Global Methodist Church). Jerry preached from Philippians 1. He began by saying that he was glad to be back but "I am so sorry for the situation that came about for why I am here. Things do change for us all the time. This is life. But God is the same God."

After an opening illustration from "Southern gospel music," Jerry preached the most Wesleyan-Sanctificationist sermon heard at Buncombe Street in the last decade, stressing the active work of God in our lives to bring to completion what God has begun in us. A strong, hopeful, redemptive, and distinctively, wonderfully Wesleyan word from Jesus, through Jerry, to the folk of my home church.

Next Sunday, January 12, Jerry followed with another truly Wesleyan, biblical sermon in which he warmly, graciously defended Wesleyan views against Calvinist predestination, though nobody at The Table seemed to mind. It sort of felt like new, allegedly independent Buncombe Street was, for good or ill, drifting back toward the church I remembered.

As a campus minister for two decades, I worry that some young Buncombe Streeter, fed a sermonic limited diet at The Table, will grow to have doubts about the veracity and reality of the rapture, a physically located heaven and hell, Satan, eternal fire for the damned, perils of Halloween, a wrathful God, and come to doubt the reality of loving Jesus Christ. I wish Justin had allowed Duke Divinity and his fellow United Methodist pastors to offer him a more robust Wesleyan theology. I would love to have read the Old Testament with him and to share my own testimonial to a gracious, salvific son of David.

And yet, . . . *what if the preaching at Buncombe Street is the future and mine is past?* I know for sure that the Lord's word endureth forever (1 Pet 1:25), even if my words, and my ways of delivering the Word, don't (Isa 40:8). As longtime Duke teacher of preachers Rick Lischer and I showed in our *Concise Encyclopedia of Preaching*, the proclamation of the church has—thank you, Holy Spirit—adapted in every age.

Reducing the dynamic, expansive, uncontainable gospel of Jesus Christ to cute quips or catchy proverbs, unarguable assertions, somber threats, or a surefire formula for choosing your way into God's heart has been tried before and found wanting, but maybe it's gospel enough—if you live in the right part of Greenville and, because you've been so successful in business and politics, are confident that you're able to set things right between you and God *if* you publicly confess your sins, take Jesus Christ as your personal savior, and claim your once-saved-always-saved ticket to eternity.

I'm not much on Emily Lynch Cupelli's praise song music at The Table. She seems to be a fine contemporary musician with a wonderfully reassuring voice, but I can't hear anyone in the congregation singing along with Emily. Most of the songs are impossible for congregational singing.

Music at The Table, from what I observe, is mostly people standing, sometimes swaying, as they listen to songs sung by the performing musicians. That's a radical innovation in Methodist worship, a liturgical tradition based in congregational singing. One of the first books published in America was printed in Charleston, South Carolina: *Collection of Psalms and Hymns*, 1737.

I wonder: Is a radically individualized, personalized gospel, accompanied by congregational division and exclusionary voting what's predictably produced when you try to worship Jesus solo? Turn worship music into a spectator sport, refit Jesus so that he's interested only in your personal sins, next thing you know, you've got people confused into thinking this is all just between me and Jesus and to heck with everybody else.

To paraphrase Dr. R. Bryce Herbert's gospel word to us confirmands so long ago: the whole point of these ceremonials is to get everyone singing from the same words and music.

And yet . . . if the choice is between the death of a congregation or the hymns of Charles Wesley, maybe it's best to give Charles a decent burial and move on. When I think of all that church planter Paul went through to help his churches to tomorrow, I bet Paul would say, "Beware the bishop who closed fifty churches in Alabama when he complains about somebody's lousy hermeneutics. At least Buncombe Street's leadership is determined to keep a downtown, mainline congregation afloat. That's better than Willimon."

You think John Wesley would bless a church with a median age of sixty-six (The UMC)? For whatever misgivings Wesley might have over the doctrine preached at The Table, the generational mix that Justin achieved there would surely warm Old Daddy's heart.

And besides, God worked through the muddled, Methodist (sort of) message that I was fed in my childhood and youth and found a way to save me (yet still on my way to perfection) in spite of the garbled gospel that was presented to me by hometown evangelists. I believe the Lord can do the same at the new Buncombe Street and at Open Hearts too. There's never been a church that's "independent" from the Holy Spirit, never been a congregation that's progressed beyond dependency upon a God who loves to raise the dead and make a way when we thought there was none.

Like I told them stuck-up New England liberals in my Beecher Lectures at Yale, thank God that I'm powerless, in even the worst of my sermons, to keep the Holy Spirit from saying anything in a sermon to anybody she pleases in any way she wants.

As bishop, I spent half my time protecting churches from overbearing or irresponsible clergy, the other half protecting clergy from overburdening, ailing congregations. Respectfully I ask the leadership of Buncombe Street, and its bevy of newly ordained clergy, are you sure you can thrive "independent" from the denomination that birthed you? All the remaining staff at Buncombe Street have sidestepped denominational oversight and none of them went to a mainline Methodist seminary. Who will confront, correct, and discipline your clergy? To whom or to what body of belief and standards of conduct will your pastoral leaders be held accountable?

I admit that I'm sounding like a bishop when I say that United Methodism's supervision and support of clergy by clergy is a Wesleyan virtue. Every United Methodist pastor is watched by fellow clerics. No United Methodist congregation has to vet, hire, contract with, supervise, or fire its clergy. When it works, it's church at its most demanding and faithful.

When it doesn't—as when DSs and bishops overlooked what was being preached at Jackson Grove or Buncombe Street and cowered before a group of powerful, politically savvy legal bullies, then in a succession of senior pastor appointments sent inadequate pastoral leadership to a prominent church, and refused to be helpful in a congregational fight—it's sad.

Connectionalism can do better. As bishop in Bama, I participated in a gripe session in a church fellowship hall. We were having a great time cataloging what's wrong with The UMC. Then a woman blurted, "You don't know what you're talking about. This church is a gift!

"I was the victim of two demagogic, out-of-control, know-it-all, abusive preachers in a row who pranced around on stage saying Jesus-this-and-Bible-that. When I finally got the courage to leave, I vowed that I'd never again be a part of a church where preachers answer to nobody but the poor old laity."

"Will you ride around with me in Alabama and give that speech in support of my ministry as an overseer?" I asked, gratefully. "And will you whisper that in my ear early every morning so I'll be emboldened to spend my day daring to act like a bishop?"

And yet, and yet. . . . I'm the one who's long been saying that denominations, as a way of doing church, are over as we have known them. When the lay leadership of Buncombe Street said that what The UMC did or didn't do was *the* decisive, detrimental factor for the future of the congregation, their lack of knowledge of the nature of congregational growth and decline was showing. Now that the future of the congregation rests solely in their hands, maybe they will step up and address Buncombe Street's truly important internal/external challenges.

Still, I'm haunted by those disaffiliates at Buncombe Street who claimed they had to get The UMC off their back in order not to sink with The UMC. Nor will I defend the ways that The UMC overseers poorly represented connectionalism to Buncombe Street.

Duke's Mark Chaves's national study showed that the number of congregations with no denominational affiliation increased from 18 percent in 1998 to 24 percent in 2012. Larger congregations are hiring more staff without theological training or denominational credentialing. "Churches and churchgoers are aging and congregations have become less connected to denominations," says Chaves. Congregational income given to denominations has shrunk from 86 percent in 1998 to 50 percent in 2012. In all this, Justin's denominational disinterest may be a vanguard.

Newly disaffiliated Buncombe Street, I'm glad that you, for the most part, still find useful the rituals, congregational governance, a few of the hymns, and all of the doctrines, beliefs, and church buildings that you received via United Methodism. Sorry that the *Discipline* was too connectional for you to handle.

Thinking back on all the times that the larger church prompted Buncombe Street to do better, now that you've left the denomination, who will prod you to do right even when it's difficult? Dr. Moseley reminds me that Buncombe Street's denominational disease is not new. He concludes *The Buncombe Street Methodist Story* saying that "the hardest lesson Buncombe Street" has had to learn "was that it is part and parcel of the Methodist Episcopacy. It cannot be a church separate and distinct."

As evidence, prescient Dr. Moseley cites Buncombe Street's vote in the 1930s *against* shedding its Methodist Episcopal Church, South designation and the official board's vote *against* "the seating of Negroes" in the summer of 1958 (I was twelve). Dr. Moseley blamed the vote on resentment of Yankee Methodists making "'conservative' . . . synonymous with 'segregation.'"

"Thus far this vote has never been reversed," mused Moseley.

In one of his last paragraphs in his history of Buncombe Street, Dr. Moseley quotes unnamed Buncombe Streeters reacting against denominational support for civil rights activists and other social justice freaks. "Since when did we give our consent to a new church body to lobby against the right-to-work laws?" "Little by little we are yielding every right we have to boards and councils and commissions speaking from afar. I say, let's stop it." It took them until 2023, but stop it they did.

The year I graduated from high school (1964), after our MYF group participated in a city-wide Halloween "Trick-or-Treat for UNICEF" campaign, some group at Buncombe Street charged that UNICEF was, like the UN, a communist front and that whoever was responsible for seducing our unsuspecting young people to work for the UN should be punished. Luther Marchant Jr., beloved director of the Greenville YMCA (who told me that I played the sorriest basketball he ever did see), conducted a study citing the "needs of children in the world," Romans 12:10-21, and Matthew 25:44-46, to reassure Buncombe Street anti-communists that the MYF was not a tool of the Reds.

The Marchant Report was the first time I heard anyone in Greenville stand up to the Red Scare. Where would I be if those old-timey conservatives had forced out by congregational vote Luther Marchant, who braved their home-brewed McCarthyism? Luther was as right about Jesus as he was about my lack of ability in basketball.

According to Moseley, Buncombe Street anti-communists had one anti-denominational victory—a resolution to withdraw all funding from the National and World Councils of Churches as chastisement for those organizations' encouragement of "the beatniks in Mississippi in the summer of 1964."

Sixty years later (these things take time), the disaffiliates finally solved Buncombe Street's "hardest lesson." Maybe I ought to ask, "What took you so long?" to vote yourselves out of the misery caused by being tethered to Methodists?

While you disaffiliates are congratulating yourselves on your steadfast adherence to doctrine, check out Wesley's *Plain Account of Christian Perfection* (1748), where Old Daddy contends: "Orthodoxy or right opinions, is, at best, but a very slender part of religion, if . . . allowed to be any part of it at all." Though your vaunted "biblical authority" is not a term Wesley would recognize, his test for it was not adherence to the letter of the law; it was sanctificationist, going-on-to-perfection "practical Christianity": how well we live the Bible's truth in our lives. A favorite proof text of John Wesley was Matthew 7:21. Look it up. For Wesley, and his holiness preachers, right living—piety, how you treat one another in church and out—was as important as right believing.

I've frequently boasted to the Global Methodist Church, even though they aren't listening, "There's nothing you can say, as harsh, critical, and scornful about bishops, The UMC, or the present *Book of Discipline*, as contemptuous as what I've said, years before you, *in print, mind you* (except for your looney obsession with drag queens). *Rekindling the Flame. Resident Aliens. A New Connection: Reforming The United Methodist Church. Bishop. Don't Look Back.* Check 'em out."

Mr. Moseley helped me to discover that some of my denominational critique I owe to my upbringing at Buncombe Street. The major difference between me and the disaffiliates is that I never, no, not once, in my critical scorn threatened to betray my ordination vows, take everything that wasn't nailed down, and walk away from our argument, just because I couldn't force you to agree with me about Jesus.

Are you Buncombe Street secessionists surprised to hear me say that you haven't nearly enough detached yourself from the ethos of a declining denomination to assure a tomorrow for yourselves? Your vision statement, organization, programs, newsletters, sermons, and style are still too much old-line, sidelined, stale denominationalism. Simply scrubbing "United" off your sign won't take you where you want to go. You took down your UMC flag of convenience under which you sailed for so long, but you have yet to secede from many of the attitudes and practices that are choking older, white, affluent, low-participation, conservative congregations (including those of the Southern Baptists and the GMC) like you to death.

The one big idea of the GMC for the future of the church? Hey, let's start another old-line, mainline, mostly Southern, legalistic, all white, aging denomination!

Give me a break.

More than once Bishop Holston publicly admitted that he was surprised by how many Methodists had neither affection nor respect for the denomination he was leading, demonstrating that he was out of touch with his conference. All recent Gallup polls report that "religion" still means a great deal to American Protestants; denominations don't. Denomination-hopping has morphed from denominational indifference to widespread hostility toward all institutional authority.

So at General Conference in 2024, Charlotte, when a bishop betrayed her age by telling delegates, "The world is watching what we do here," I, having observed the shrinking value of the denomination and its official pronouncements and virtue-signaling conclave, muttered, "No it isn't."

Congregational disagreements over inclusiveness are nothing new. I figure that half of the New Testament is a debate over Paul's shocking claim, "God's salvation has been sent to the Gentiles" (Acts 28:28). I entered the ministry during the fight over the racial integration of The UMC, a fight we won with a vote one afternoon at annual conference in Columbia but not on Sunday morning at 11:00 at Buncombe Street in Greenville.

The denomination's 1960s white supremacists look poorly organized in comparison with the steeplejackers of 2023, though there are some troubling similarities. Only 1 of 250 disaffiliating churches in the 50 percent Black S.C. UMC is Black. The GMC is more predominantly white even than its predecessor, The UMC.

Duke's David Roso and David Eagle did an extensive study of disaffiliating clergy in North Carolina, *Disaffiliation from the United Methodist Church in North Carolina: Challenges and Opportunities.* They found that disaffiliating clergy almost exclusively identify as white, male (80 percent), an even higher percentage of clergymen than The UMC or American Protestantism as a whole. They are more likely to be licensed local pastors (like Justin) rather than elders (like Brian and all earlier Buncombe Street senior pastors).

One of my African American, South Carolina UMC clergy friends said, "Your rich white church wanted us to leave. When you found we weren't going anywhere, y'all had to disaffiliate yourselves to get rid of us."

The 1844 division of Methodism over slavery, which created The Methodist Episcopal Church, South, is sometimes cited by disaffiliates as just another historic instance of beneficial separation in Methodism. (That split took 40 percent of the membership of The Methodist Episcopal Church, whereas disaffiliations, 24 percent.) Over half of the disaffiliates came from the Southeastern Jurisdictions of The UMC, leading one wag to say, "The GMC ought to call itself the CMC, Confederate Methodist Church."

The leadership of the new Buncombe Street cover their right-wing views and social fears with appeals to Scripture. Sorry, the Bible is not your buddy in defense of lurking Trumpism.

Growing up I heard a lot of sermonic subterfuge. "It's not about race, it's about states' rights." "It's not about segregation; it's about protecting our children." "We don't have a race problem in Greenville if these outside Northern agitators would leave us alone." "It's not about politics; it's about preserving the pure word of God." I had to go to a United Methodist college to have these lies rectified.

As one observer told me, Buncombe Street's disaffiliates didn't have to be explicit about their politics; conservative Republicanism is the air Greenville breathes. Greenville is the home of rabidly fundamentalist Bob Jones University. In the last election three incumbent Republicans were defeated by even more conservative Republicans for county council. The Greenville delegation (state representatives and senators), uniformly Republican. Krista Bannister's husband, Jim, practices law with his brother Bruce, a high-ranking member of the South Carolina House of Representatives. Julie Turner's husband, Ross, is a long-serving South Carolina senator.

"They took a church conflict and turned it into a political fight, using their political skills to pull it off," charged one attorney, no friend of the disaffiliates. "The Bible was their cover for a right-wing political coup." The data from the Roso and Eagle study clearly document the right-wing Republican leanings of the disaffiliates.

While working on this memoir, I picked up James Davison Hunter's *Democracy and Solidarity: On the Cultural Roots of America's Political Crisis.* Hunter says that Americans, in the last couple of decades divided ourselves into victims and villains, oppressors and oppressed, true believers and those who are not.

In a time when many fear they're floating in a moral and social vacuum, our divisions give us a sense of belonging, says Hunter. We achieve social recognition, attract attention, grab power and influence over others, and gain self-respect by identifying and then venting rage against "them." This so-called "identity politics" is practiced equally aggressively in church by the right ("biblical authority") or left ("inclusion").

In his 1966 Greenville crusade, Billy Graham offered a wide welcome to the faith that was central to American life. By 2020 son Franklin was an armed warrior in a fierce, life-or-death battle with anti-Christian culture. Justin's battle cry, "folks, we're in a war," is a long way from the "come to Jesus" evangelists of old. And the secretive, hysterical propaganda of the Friends of Buncombe Street? Truth, war's first casualty.

While Hunter is worried about the damage that oppositional, identity politics does to democracy, my concern, by virtue of my vows, is the church. When secular political strategies and labels are baptized by a church, with the view that there are those in our own church who are out to get us and do damage to God, persuasion is for suckers. The authoritarian impulse is difficult for Jesus to restrain. Get the votes, pack committees and councils, send out anonymous emails, crush them from the top down, and then offer them the door.

The point of a political campaign is power; the point of the Christian life is love. That's why there's always friction between the two. To the disaffiliates I say, while you're busy fixing the church, using the political skills you learned in the new GOP, you are not free to trash the Sermon on the Mount. Or disregard Jesus's commands to love. To dismember the body of Christ on the basis of politics, of the right or the left, is a terrible sin.

The disaffiliates did a remarkable job of coaxing the congregation to focus exclusively on denominational factors beyond Buncombe Street, presenting them as life-and-death determinants for the future of the congregation. Buncombe Street is just fine, except for our attachment to The UMC.

Many of the disaffiliates said that their model was just a few blocks from Buncombe Street, on West Washington, mighty, longtime conservative First Presbyterian. (You may recall First Pres was cited by Fred in his manifesto.) There are those who suspect that their prototype was

Grace Church, farther down the street on West McBee. Evangelical, independent, rip-roaring, fundamentalist.

Disaffiliationists profited from a divided, Manichaean, contentious, suspicious, anti-institutional, conspiracy theory, us-versus-them America. The years 2021–2023 were a golden age for schism, division, and the separation of the goats from the sheep, good fish from the bad, wheat from the tares, even though Jesus gives scant justification for doing so. Name-calling, division of "us" and "them" worked well in the disaffiliationists' we're-in-a-war-with-the-world, preacher-always-knows rework of the gospel just as it led to their success in the 2024 elections. Having ridden in on this particular cultural moment, what will you do when the culture changes?

"It's going to take us years to get our party back," a long-term South Carolina Republican leader confided. "We're trying to figure out how to have a future, now that these personality cult, right-wing wackos hijacked our party."

If disaffiliates were uncomfortable with disagreement among Buncombe Streeters, the new Buncombe Street should please them. The Roso and Eagle study of the two North Carolina UMC conferences after disaffiliation found exiting clergy tended to be homogeneous in their political orientations and reported that their re-formed congregations, having excluded their few "progressives," were now pretty much all on the same page. Church as echo chamber. Nearly all (94 percent) of leaving N.C. clergy were white, and most were local pastors—like Buncombe Street's ministerial staff. (Still, that their preachers keep begging for "unity" in their sermons suggests that somebody is still left at Buncombe Street who has the guts to disagree.)

Unlike the emerging Global Methodist Church, the reconstituted UMC, at least in North Carolina, is politically and theologically more diverse. Based on clergy's assessments of their own congregations, 59 percent of remaining UMC congregations were evenly divided between Republican and Democratic members. "Clearly, those who left were almost universally conservative politically and theologically. But those staying were more mixed," said the Duke researchers. That means that UMC debates over matters like human sexuality will likely continue, requiring UMC clergy to get better at curating church arguments and deliberations, and making The UMC one of the few institutions left in America where people from different political persuasions connect and debate without forcing dissenters out of the discussion.

I'm talking about you, Open Hearts. Embrace your future.

I'd like to see The UMC claim our ideological divides as opportunities to test whether or not Jesus Christ makes possible togetherness in ways that the US Constitution does not. Had you the interest, and I the time, I could make a case that if there are deeply divisive issues, unmentionable hot-button questions, they cannot, should not be discussed anywhere but in church. Let's reclaim the wonder of being part of a people who are able to say, "Let's have an honest, no-holds-barred argument, speak honestly and listen intensely, under the pledge that after our knock-down debate we'll go to the Lord's Table and partake of his Body and Blood *together*. Now, let's talk."

I wonder if things would have turned out differently for my home church if, instead of calling their main service The Table, they would have called it The *Lord's* Table; everyone (even the most difficult) is at Christ's table for only one reason: this gathering is the Lord's idea of a good time.

In my classes at Duke, I say, "It's 'mission' whenever the gospel is taken across human borders and boundaries." The church grows (see Matt 28:19-20) not by hunkering behind our barricades but by reaching across the aisle, disrespecting national borders, and talking to people who have no interest in talking with us. You can't do evangelism in an echo chamber.

In his *Large Minutes,* 1784, when Methodism in America was established, Bishop Asbury asked, "What may we reasonably believe to be God's design in raising up the Preachers called Methodists?" Answer: "To reform the Continent, and spread scriptural Holiness over these Lands." Proof? "We have seen in the Course of Fifteen Years a great and glorious Work of God, from New York through the Jersies, Pennsylvania, Delaware, Maryland, Virginia, North and South Carolina, even to Georgia."

"Scriptural Holiness," lives reformed and guided by the living word, not "biblical authority" or even salvation or decisions for Christ, but the outward, missionary movement of embodied Christian love "even to Georgia."

Hey, new Buncombe Street, how will you be faithful to the Great Commission now that you've pushed out of the discussion those who disagree with your biblical interpretation or diverge on the one-issue-that's-not-the-only-issue? Doesn't evangelism involve persuasion? You're not off to a great start by using the worldly means of a ballot to expel those whom you lack the wherewithal to convert.

A large UMC congregation in South Carolina was considering whether or not to go Global Methodist. The GMC bishop was dispatched to talk them into it. During the discussion, an older adult member asked, "Will we still be able to support Epworth?" (the beloved UMC children's home in Columbia).

"No," said the bishop, "because Epworth allows gay couples to adopt their children."

"What kind of church opposes orphans having parents adopt them?" the Methodist asked in astonishment. His congregation stayed UMC.

What will be Buncombe Street's rallying cry when a majority of Americans, including even those attending The Table, eventually discover that the Lord doesn't have much at stake in opposing same-sex relationships? My read on present trends gives you less than a decade on that one.

"Granddaddy, our church split from the denomination and changed its name because of *that*?"

Try your but-that-wasn't-the-only-reason and see if it works. If you're still having Bible studies, I'm sure some youth will say, "Show me in the Bible where that's a big issue."

After having detached yourselves from one set of external forces (the leftward lean of United Methodism, bishops, the "gay agenda," drag queens, financial apportionments to pay for denominational mission), now the leadership of the new Buncombe Street must tackle the more difficult (and more relevant) task of asking the question you have, through all of your energy expended on disaffiliation, avoided: "What do we need to do, right here in our time and place, to give our church a future?" That's the one thing Congregationalists get right. I suspect you've given far too much weight to institutional, external factors, convincing yourselves that the denomination is very, very important in determining the future of your congregation.

It is not and never has been. Having disposed of the bishop and The UMC, now there's nobody to blame but yourselves. If you take it and break it, you own it.

The Lord may have raptured me, or at least taken my breath away by then, but if United Methodists were allowed to bet, I'd bet that by the time Buncombe Street turns two hundred, all mention of the evil of same-sex love will have vanished. If you succeed in getting your membership to read the Bible, some of them will discover that Jesus is not as hung up on hell as you. You'll need a plan B.

Readers will recall that disaffiliates warned the congregation that if they didn't vote to disaffiliate, expensive litigation would result. They also repeatedly reassured everyone that the millions in the various Buncombe Street endowments would be securely and uncontestedly in the hands of the new independent Buncombe Street.

They obviously didn't know, as well as I, those formidable sisters, Mary Frances and Martha Frances Morgan. Both sisters gave their lives to teaching (intimidating?) Greenville's young and to supporting (petrifying?) the clergy of Buncombe Street. Many were the nights I awoke in a sweat, even into my thirties, forties, shaking with fear because of my nightmare, hearing again the death knell in Miss Martha Frances Morgan's command: "Willimon. Go to the board and conjugate *pugnare*." Even one mistake in the pluperfect would lead Miss Morgan to drop her head and sigh to my trembling classmates, "Alas, in life, some move ahead, some don't. Will, take your seat."

I saw a high school football tackle fall to his knees, crying like a baby, begging to be allowed to go to the boys room to blow his nose, vowing to Miss Morgan that he would never again sink so low as to butcher a sentence from Cicero.

Mary Frances Morgan was said to be less fierce in the classroom, though my mother said that both sisters ruthlessly dictated all things in the Aldersgate Sunday School Class and none of the women dared to protest.

Dr. Bryan Crenshaw once confided to me that he had been "battered almost beyond recognition" by "those two harpies" just for failing to name them to the Lake Junaluska Dam Fund Committee.

One Sunday night, after I had preached that morning at Stuart Auditorium, Lake Junaluska, Bishop Tullis (now in retirement at the lake) called me hooting, "You may have impressed a lot of people, but you're still on probation with the Morgans. I opined to Martha Frances that I enjoyed your sermon. She replied, 'It was adequate. Not one grammatical error, surprisingly. Willimon was, in spite of his mother, a rather indifferent student, as I recall.'"

"I was sixteen years old!" was my only defense. Miss Morgan, God bless her, teacher forever.

Just before their deaths, the sisters gave their entire estate to establish the Frank Burt Morgan and Ethel Robinson Morgan Fund in memory of their parents. The fund demonstrated the sisters' deep, lifetime devotion to The United Methodist Church. Sixty percent of the proceeds from their endowment were to support the denomination's Intentional Growth Center at their beloved Lake Junaluska, 40 percent to charitable activities and worthy guest teachers at Buncombe Street United Methodist Church.

The legal documentation for their fund also showed the sisters' savvy. If either beneficiary "no longer exists or fails to qualify as an organization," 100 percent of the fund's proceeds shall go to the other beneficiary.

Few at Buncombe Street were informed that, in late 2023, the Intentional Growth Center told Buncombe Street—a church ruled by the bishop as officially dead but now, with deed in hand, resurrected as the new, independent, soon to be Global Methodist Buncombe Street—"see you in court."

Are other endowments at the new church at risk?

The staff of both Buncombe Street and Open Hearts seemed nervous about my interviewing their members. Both characterized their congregations as "still hurting," "just beginning to heal," and "vulnerable." The last thing they needed was a has-been bishop poking around, talking about matters wished left unsaid. Bishop Holston avoided returning my calls.

Maybe it's because I'm a preacher, but I believe that silence is rarely a virtue, never if it's in service of concealment. Jesus was not crucified for his times of silent, solitary prayer. He would have never been nailed to a cross if he had been argument averse. I don't know everything I'd like to know about the dynamics of Buncombe Street's disaffiliation but I'm sure that the disaffiliation breakup was made worse by the silence of the bishop, DS, and pastors. They attributed their muteness to their graciousness; I've got another name for it.

I'm untroubled that the disaffiliates raised questions, made charges, recycled trash from the Institute on Religion and Democracy, or unfairly criticized The United Methodist Church. I'm sad that The United Methodist Church lacked the courage to care enough for the state of the souls under their care, or the future of Buncombe Street to stand up to the disaffiliates and say "you're wrong."

Looking back on my years at Buncombe Street as a youth, during the days of Greenville's legally enforced racial segregation, I wish that some pastor had risked controversy, conflict, and schism by foregoing silence and openly discussing race like a Christian, in spite of the cost of speaking up. I'd give anything to be able to point to one instance of a preacher saying something on race that the congregation wished he hadn't.

I can't.

It's ironic that my home church split, causing a number of members to feel forced forever out of the church they helped to build, under the guise of "unity" and "togetherness." At the meeting just before the vote, we heard the pastors take turns begging the congregation to vote to disaffiliate in order to heal a church "torn apart" by all this "mess." Church unity was bought at a high price—consolidating power in the hands of a few, driving out of the discussion and disempowering any Methodist who didn't talk a lot like a Baptist.

It's a reminder that Christ's notion of "unity" is very different from that of the world.

Neither the bishop nor anybody at Buncombe Street noted Acts 15, the so-called "Jerusalem Council." What to do about these gentiles who, in spite of the many biblical texts that say gentiles have no part in the promises of God to Israel, still show up asking, "Can I be included in Christ's salvation?" Should they be required to submit to Jewish purity codes and circumcision? God's word clearly demands it. The Bible says it. Most of our leaders and the majority of the congregation believe it. Shouldn't that settle it?

In the first recorded church fight in history, there is no proof-texting from the Old Testament and no vote is taken. What's said is that "it seemed good to the Holy Spirit and to us," to make adjustments to the application of biblical requirements so that the gentiles could be baptized. Christ's expansive salvation for all overrules any other consideration. How I love that discretionary, humble, it *seemed* good. The leaders of Buncombe Street took another path.

By my count, easily a third of the content of Paul's letters deals with the problems of divisive conflict in his missionary congregations. Paul's injunction to forbear (*anekhómenoi*, tolerate, put up with) one another in love (Col 3:13; Eph 4:2) should have been done in needlepoint, framed, and put over the front door of Buncombe Street UMC. Not the door at the top of the front steps almost nobody uses, the one at the side that leads from the parking lot across the street into the cramped hallway through which Mother and I always entered.

> As a prisoner for the Lord, I encourage you to live as people worthy of the call you received from God. . . . Accept each other with love, and make an effort to preserve the unity of the Spirit with the peace that ties you together. You are one body and one spirit, just as God also called you in one hope. There is one Lord, one faith, one baptism, and one God and Father of all, who is over all, through all, and in all. (Eph 4:1-6)

Paul's letters are packed with conflicted, contentious discussion. There's no congregational fight among his congregations where Paul doesn't want a piece of the action. Quiescent, cowering Methodist bishops take note: Paul never backs down from arguing with congregational opponents. The gospel makes him do it. And yet, never, ever does Paul say, "Since I can't convince you, I'm leaving," or "You are so closed and conservative, you're beyond persuasion," much less, "This church would be better off if you would quietly go away."

Above all, for the Christian congregation, togetherness, unity within diversity, forbearance of one another in love are not merely signs of adept pastoral leadership and a healthy church; *koinonia*, worshipping and serving Christ *together* is the whole point of church in the first place, a good unto itself, a necessary demonstration of what Jesus Christ is up to. Separation, division, exclusion, and congregational voting have never received encouragement from Scripture.

Thank God a score of African American Methodists refused to cease *anekhómenoi* me and didn't say, "His home church is Buncombe Street; God will never change his mind." Thank goodness those who, when I was young, wanted to take my home church away from the denomination weren't given that opportunity before God, working through The UMC, had time to work on them and me.

How different might have been all that transpired at Buncombe Street if the pastor, DS, anybody, had begun by asking everybody to stand, raise right hands, and repeat the words, "I promise to speak honestly, listen carefully, and then *to put up with one another* no matter who offends me." Instead, they disobeyed Paul's clear, biblical injunction to *anekhómenoi* one another and fought like Republicans and Democrats, conservatives and progressives, pushing opponents out of the party rather than putting up with them as those whom Christ had put at his table. When Paul wrestled with the most divided, contentious, culturally accommodated congregation ever, First Church Corinth, he didn't tell them to read their Bibles, go by Roberts Rules of Order, choose up sides, lawyer up, share what's on their hearts, put it to a vote, or even to pray. Instead, he urged them to join in singing:

> Love is patient, love is kind, it isn't jealous, it doesn't brag, it isn't arrogant, it isn't rude, it doesn't seek its own advantage, it isn't irritable, it

doesn't keep a record of complaints, it isn't happy with injustice, but it is happy with the truth. Love puts up with all things, trusts in all things, hopes for all things, endures all things. Love never fails. As for prophecies, they will be brought to an end. As for tongues, they will stop. As for knowledge, it will be brought to an end. . . . Now faith, hope, and love remain—these three things—and the greatest of these is love. (1 Cor 13:4-8, 13)

Read Justin's Erskine dissertation on 1 Corinthians. He'll convince you that Christians believe, on the basis of pastor Paul, it's better to be in relationship than to be right, better to continue to argue with one another than to push anybody out of a conversation into which the living Christ promises to intrude. Where just two or three of us are gathered, even fighting like cats and dogs over whatever causes us discomfort in Jesus's boundless evangelical embrace, Christ says, "Count me in" (Matt 18:20).

I adore that they celebrate the Eucharist every Sunday at The Table. Good for them. Their open table is about the most defiantly non-Baptist thing they do. "Open table," in historic Methodism, means that we don't sit in judgment upon, nor do we take votes on excluding anybody whom Jesus has invited to drink his cup of salvation. Or as Wesley argued, this isn't a supper reserved for the certified saints, it's a "converting ordinance" for all who are open to Christ's transformative, sanctifying love.

On January 19, 2025, Chris Ashley opened his sermon on Ephesians 4 saying, "in the last two months we have had a crash course in being the church. However, we have also been given the opportunity of a reset." Chris then gave a passionate plea for "unity" at Buncombe Street as the greatest need in a congregational "reset," making me wonder what divisions still persisted. Buncombe Street had been promised that, if we vote out those who wish to stay UMC, we'll at last be unified.

I also noted a slump in attendance, suggesting that though Justin's name was no longer mentioned, his preaching was deeply missed.

You may recall that Justin's first act as senior pastor was to press the board to tuck the Traditional Service into the 8:30 a.m. time slot in order to showcase The Table at 11:00 a.m. The March 18 congregational newsletter announced, "An **11:00 am Traditional Service** will be added to our Sunday morning worship schedule starting Sunday, April 27. There will also be a special dedication in our Orders Prayer Garden that Sunday for Rev. Dr. Justin Gilreath and a tribute in our worship services."

Buncombe Street was either falling back into its old, comfortable past or moving on. I couldn't say for sure.

————

While I was at work on *The Church We Carry*, Eliza Griswold's *Circle of Hope: A Reckoning with Love, Power, and Justice in an American Church* appeared, a study of a thriving liberal, innovative, justice-loving, Bible-questioning church that disintegrated. Circle of Hope and Buncombe Street are polar opposites in every way except one. Both congregations decided that it's okay to lose church members in pursuit of some presumably greater good that's more important than Christ-mandated togetherness.

Circle of Hope was willing to divide and die fighting for gay inclusion. Buncombe Street was prepared to live without a significant portion of its longtime membership, so determined was it to win the war against gay inclusion. Both congregations were dead wrong to disregard Paul's command to *anekhómenoi* one another in love.

Caucusing with like-minded Christians, easy. Church, hard.

After retiring from the episcopacy, I served an urban congregation for a wonderful year. I was followed by a pastor whose chief theological conviction was that Jesus died for gender inclusion. She pushed the church to vote to become a Reconciling Congregation, fly a rainbow flag, began every service with the laborious recitation of a long Statement of Welcome to a rapidly dwindling congregation. In just a couple of years this historic, downtown congregation welcomed only a handful of LGBTQIA+ Christians, far fewer than the number of Methodists driven away by the pastor's single-issue, you're-either-on-my-side-or-the-outside politics. The few mostly older white women left in the congregation are now exploring how to sell the building. Being a church that's half as welcoming as Jesus to *all* those whom he desires to save has never been easy.

Whenever leaders of a congregation decide that some good is paramount to being in communion with that gaggle of sinners whom Christ has assembled as his body in this part of his world in order to save the whole world, church disaffiliates from the reconciling, gathering mission of Christ. The sin of Buncombe Street was not in their disagreement, contentiousness, or fierce advocacy of the revelation that had been given to them. The offense was in the vote, in the public, official, majority vote that told fellow Christians, "We are quite willing to be the body of Christ without you."

I'll admit it: It's easy for me to come up with reasons and factors that explain why a church like Buncombe Street would divide and splinter. Sociology, psychology, and economics offer excellent explanations for human disunion. Congregational dissension and division come naturally. We were born to go our own way and to say to heck with everybody else.

More difficult is to explain why there was a Buncombe Street Church in the first place. No other explanation for that communal wonder than one that's biblical, theological. Only reference to a determinedly convening Jesus accounts for why, in spite of all the perfectly natural human reasons why not, there ever was a Buncombe Street Church.

"You're welcome," says Jesus.

———————

December 4, 2024, I received an email from a leader of the Global Methodist Church who said he had heard that I was writing a book about the Buncombe Street disaffiliation: "Your arrogance and need to write yet another book have put yourself first, ahead of others. That's not what Jesus meant when He commanded us to love our neighbors as ourselves."

The writer claimed to be a close friend of Justin's (untrue) and bragged that he had extensively consulted with the lay leadership of Buncombe Street as leader in the Wesleyan Covenant Association (true). He charged that I had been asked to cease conversation with people at Buncombe Street and I had callously refused (untrue). I was never asked by anyone, least of all Justin, not to contact folks at my home church.

Justin often said that he could not care less about denominations, a sentiment in line with his youthful outlook, telling people that he didn't mind, one way or another, if the new Buncombe Street affiliated with a denomination.

By early January 2025 I realized why this GMC critic had written me. In an announcement that surprised no one, the denominational affiliation committee announced that the disaffiliating church council and all the church staff had recommended affiliation with the Global Methodist Church. A series of "Listening Sessions" was to be held prior to a "churchwide vote." Why the GMC? The chief advantages of this new denomination, arising from the wreckage of the old, were explained:

- Authority of Scripture

- Support and accountability for clergy and staff

- BSMC will have final decision on clergy selection and can search worldwide if needed

- Powershift from denomination to local church

- We own property/endowments, apportionments reduced from 16% to 4%, and easy disaffiliation if needed

In the promotional video, Krista Bannister said, "We believe the Global Methodist Church aligns with our theology and vision." "We believe it goes back to Charles Wesley's [sic] roots . . . without all the bureaucracy."

Apparently, word was out that I was working on this book, causing trepidation among the leaders of the GMC. On a podcast in January 2025, a once-UMC local pastor, now a proud "Global Methodist Elder," delivered a long jeremiad titled, "Bucombe [sic] Street Methodist Voting on GMC After Being **Targeted** by Bishop Willimon." He dismissed me as "churlish."

Not to sound churlish but, dear polemicist, at least spell the church's name right.

The GMC need not have been alarmed. On February 9, 2025, 485 remaining members of Buncombe Street (less than one-fourth of the congregation's total membership) voted by a margin of 98 percent to become Global Methodists.

Years of careful, cagey work by representatives of the Wesleyan Covenant Association and the Global Methodist Church had paid off. A large, historic church, now vulnerable and without a senior pastor, had fallen into the waiting arms of the GMC.

Knowing how little denominational labels meant for the congregation's future, I wondered how Justin would have greeted the February vote.

We'll never know.

Krista Bannister had promised Buncombe Street that "BSMC will have final decision on clergy selection and can search worldwide if needed." As soon as the church became GMC, Krista began a search free of the constraints of a UMC bishop.

It was early May before the church newsletter announced, "Buncombe Street Welcomes Pastor Lonnie Pittman."

After serving small congregations in Alabama, Lonnie had transferred to the Western North Carolina Conference where he had a series of short-term appointments. When his Mount Tabor UMC congregation was stunned to discover Lonnie's name on a list of Global Methodist pastors, Lonnie's bishop insisted that he be public and truthful about his allegiances. Blaming his exposure as a GMC operative on an "egregious clerical error," in his farewell letter to the congregation, Lonnie admitted, "I have been drifting from the UMC for a while (and they from me)" and complained that the bishop had "forced me out." "I do not have a job," pled Lonnie, now desperately looking for a church and insurance, though grateful that his family was allowed to stay in the parsonage until the end of the year.

The GMC appointed Lonnie to dwindling Central Methodist Church in Asheboro, North Carolina, average attendance less than two hundred. From Asheboro, Lonnie was called to Buncombe Street.

Lonnie's wife, Susanna, also ordained, served a string of short-term appointments on church staffs in North Carolina. Both were known for feeling under-appreciated by The UMC (a frequent complaint of GMC pastors).

Buncombe Street has handed the Pittmans a daunting task.

———————

While I'll leave you to draw theological conclusions and church leadership lessons for your particular context, here are a few things that may merit your continued reflection:

- Congregationalism, independence, and disconnection come naturally. Connectionalism, as a way of doing church, is countercultural and difficult to sustain.

- Episcopal oversight and clergy appointment by a bishop, though biblical and historic, is tough in North America. Pastors who are willing to be sent, and bishops who make informed, careful assessment of clergy and congregations are a Wesleyan dream that's hard to realize in an anti-institutional, individualistic, capitalist context.

- Wesleyan Christianity, as God's gift to the world, requires constant refurbishment and indoctrination. It's easier to divide the world into the saved and the unsaved, elect and damned, truly committed and merely casual believers, progressives and conservatives than to extrovertedly preach Wesleyan "Salvation for all!"

- Sometimes, claims of graciousness and love are the way that we clergy cover our lack of leadership daring.

- Some clergy conceal their desire for power over others with claims that what they say is out of love for their people, what the Bible says, or what Jesus told them he wants.

- To invoke any other value or noble goal as more important than invitation to commune together at Christ's table and enjoy the communal benefits of one Lord, one faith, one baptism is to have misunderstood Jesus.

- Pastors are community persons whose primary job is to care about and work for what makes for community among the odd cast of characters Jesus Christ has died to save and is determined to assemble, otherwise known as church.

- Preachers submit our lives to priestly listening of Scripture, disciplining ourselves to talk about what Jesus wants to talk about rather than what nine out of ten Americans would like to hear.

- Whenever we take up the sword, using worldly political means, slogans, and power plays to defend Jesus, we betray our Lord's way of having his kingdom come, his will to be done on earth as in heaven.

- If your doctrinal commitments make it hard for you to put up with fellow Christians at the Lord's Table, you may have given too much of yourself to questionable doctrines.

- Go ahead and love Jesus but remember that other Christians will love him differently than you.

- While we might like to hit people over the head with the Bible and then, when we fail to convert them to our opinions, vote them out of the fellowship, that's not Jesus's way of doing things.

- Anybody who's afraid of or doesn't know how to curate arguments, manage conflict, protect a congregation from bullies, and speak the truth in love shouldn't be a pastor, much less a bishop or district superintendent.

- Leadership that's good at dividing, winning, and seizing power is rarely competent to create, convene, and grow a church. Those who are good at fomenting a revolution are rarely good at doing the dishes.

Maybe our Lord is habituated to being disappointed by the disrepair of his body, unsurprised by the tale I have told about my home church. From the beginning, church has never lived up to his expectation, requiring Christ to show up repeatedly and build back his body that we have abused. Every church is different from the church Jesus intends. So we must forever submit to being, "His new creation by water and the Word," as Samuel Wesley coaxed us to sing, church dying and rising and rising again.

Catch my allusion to "The Church's One Foundation," Number 545 in *The United Methodist Hymnal*? I heard it sung so often at Buncombe Street that, as a Boy Scout, I even learned to play it on my harmonica. I insisted it be sung at my installations as Dean of the Chapel at Duke and again when I became a bishop in 'Bama.

In the videos I've watched, I haven't heard "The Church's One Foundation" sung at the new Buncombe Street, but they should. Now, more than ever.

> The Church's one foundation
> is Jesus Christ her Lord;
> he is his new creation
> by water and the Word.
> From heaven he came and sought her
> to be his holy bride;
> with his own blood he bought her,
> and for her life he died.

The hymn was written by Anglican bishop Samuel John Stone in South Africa amid a nasty church fight in the 1860s, when Buncombe Street was still a new church plant. It's a riff on 1 Corinthians 3:11, Christ the Foundation. The hymn premiered at the 1868 Lambeth Conference (the same year that Greenvillians realized they had lost the Civil War). The tune is the beloved "Aurelia" by Samuel Sebastian Wesley, grandson of Charles, whose hymns Buncombe Street doesn't sing much anymore, though I wish they would.

Stone wrote "The Church's One Foundation" as a slap in the face to Bishop John William Colenso, first bishop of Natal, who was being deposed for his heretical teaching that Moses didn't really write the Pentateuch. Bishop Colenso clung to his historical/critical views, scorning oversight by fellow bishops. Would Colenso bolt and start his own church? Schism was in the air. Thus the takedown of Bishop Colenso in the third stanza:

> Though with a scornful wonder
> we see her sore oppressed,
> by schisms rent asunder,
> by heresies distressed,
> yet saints their watch are keeping;
> their cry goes up, "How long?"
> And soon the night of weeping
> shall be the morn of song.

The United Methodist Hymnal has wisely omitted original stanza three, where Stone takes off the gloves and goes after Bishop Colenso tooth, claw, and nail:

> The Church shall never perish!
> her dear Lord to defend,
> To guide, sustain, and cherish,
> is with her to the end;
> Though there be those who hate her,
> and false sons in her pale,
> Against or foe or traitor
> she ever shall prevail.

But then the hymn moves from name calling and score settling to redemption by Christ:

> 'Mid toil and tribulation,
> and tumult of her war,
> she waits the consummation
> of peace for evermore;
> till, with the vision glorious,
> her longing eyes are blest,

and the great church victorious
shall be the church at rest.

Yet she on earth hath union
with God the Three in One,
and mystic sweet communion
with those whose rest is won.
O happy ones and holy!
Lord, give us grace that we
like them, the meek and lowly,
on high may dwell with thee.

"The church shall never perish," not because we've at last assembled visionary lay leadership or, in spite of the bishop, we've got the prominent preacher we deserve, or we are serious about the Bible, finally. It's not up to the church, "her dear Lord to defend." Thank goodness United Methodists left original stanza three out of the hymnal. Defense, renovation, and reassembling of the poor old church are Jesus's self-assigned tasks. "Mid toil and tribulation, and tumult of her war," convening Jesus is unwilling for our story finally to be a separationist tragedy. No matter how we botch the song he wants us to sing, he insists on writing a joyful last verse, turning our lament into hallelujah. Though the church messes up and falls short of Christ's expectations, he keeps showing up and taking matters in hand, so determined in Jesus to have us in his "mystic sweet communion." Together.

Therein is hope.

Postlude

I sat in my car on Richardson, beside Buncombe Street, lucky to have found a parking space on a Sunday at 10:30 a.m. For the first time I noticed that an impressive array of church buildings had usurped the place where once sat Dr. Herbert's Plymouth as well as our beloved BSA Troop Nine Scout Hut. I wish the Hut—with the mural I painted on the wall outside the Scoutmaster's office of the Cherokee Ghost Dancer, and the big fireplace, and the knuckleheaded Tenderfoot Scouts—was still there.

I watched young couples, families, people of all ages, really, some of them almost running, surging toward the entrance to The Table. All were white, well-dressed, eager, surprisingly so. Many clutched Bibles.

In no more than a few dozen downtown, large United Methodist churches is this scene unfolding. I was shaken by a thought, maybe inserted by the Holy Spirit: *what if, like John on Patmos, I'm seeing the future?*

By 10:45, every parking space was taken. My coffee cup was empty, but Buncombe Street Global Methodist Church looked full. I didn't go in. Yes, I'm sore because of their demolition of the Scout Hut to make way for the big building John Redmond and his banished Buncombe Streeters built and paid for to house The Table. But my main reason for holding back is that seeing my home church resolutely trash both my memories and the Methodism that built it makes me feel out of place in the present, averse to what I see of tomorrow.

Annie Dillard, telling a group of us what she learned writing her *An American Childhood*, warned that memoir is the worst way "to preserve your memories. If you prize your memories as they are . . . avoid . . . writing a memoir. Because it is in a certain way to lose them. You can't put together a memoir without cannibalizing your own life for parts. The work batters your memoires. And it replaces them."

How true.

Maybe I didn't join them at The Table because of my pride, my snootiness. Or maybe it was fear that there I might meet Christ in a way that would make me uncomfortable, that I would encounter practices that call into question how Jesus has worked me for seven decades. I don't know. It would be just like Jesus to show up in the midst of someone's grief, messing with memories, in a guise that makes the mourner uneasy.

So I did what people my age are supposed to do. I left.

I started my car, fastened my seat belt, and pulled into the street, leaving forever the church that once bore me, or maybe, according to Hebrews 13:14, a perishable place that failed to live up to my reminiscence. Whether I was leaving the church that I have borne, or through the backward view watching my church leave me, I can't say for sure.

It could be a rough ride home.

I went down Richardson, took a left on Buncombe, headed east, out of town, back to Durham, returning to a church more congruent with my tastes, a theology more congenial with someone at my age and stage, huddled with a few superannuated Christians, some sad or mad, a few hopeful, all supposed to be looking for a church "that is still to come."

Just before turning onto Buncombe, in my rearview mirror I saw a Range Rover filled with a young family, thrilled that Jesus had answered their prayers for parking, glad to take up the church I was putting down, joyful to be arriving at the church that I was leaving.

Or the church that left me.

Acknowledgments

When a handful of wholly committed human beings give themselves fully to a great cause or faith they are virtually irresistible. They cut through the partial and fleeting commitments of the rest of society like a buzz saw through peanut brittle.

—*Dean Kelley,* Why Conservative Churches Are Growing

As I prepared to write, I watched available videos from Buncombe Street 2022–2025, including all of Justin Gilreath's sermons, read the church council minutes, the presentations of the Way Forward Task Force and the Save Our Legacy group, labored in the Wofford archives, and conducted more than two hundred phone interviews and group listening sessions.

Books in congregational studies, especially Nancy Ammerman's *Studying Congregations: A New Handbook*, tutored me in research methodology for studying churches like Buncombe Street and Open Hearts.[1]

Slice Penny provided assistance in collecting and sorting interviews. Kate Bowler, Lauren Winner, Grant Wacker, Rick Lischer, Daniel Castello, Curtis Freeman, David Eagle, and Mark Chaves of Duke Divinity School encouraged and advised me. As with all of my projects, I couldn't have done it without the guidance of fourth-generation Methodist and former member of Trinity on Augusta Street Patsy Parker Willimon.

---

1. Nancy T. Ammerman, Jackson W. Carroll, Carl S. Dudley, and William McKinney, *Studying Congregations: A New Handbook* (Nashville: Abingdon Press, 1998).

I had planned to list the names of the more than two hundred people who helped me better understand Buncombe Street, Methodists, united or not. Because some of them feared retribution or censure, I've removed their names. I'm all the more grateful that they loved the church enough to talk to me.

www.ingramcontent.com/pod-product-compliance
Lightning Source LLC
LaVergne TN
LVHW011245200625
813984LV00008B/15